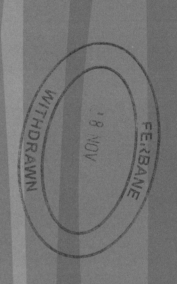

HOOKED

Adventures in Angling & Eating

MARK HIX

MITCHELL BEAZLEY

An Hachette UK Company
www.hachette.co.uk

First published in Great Britain in 2019 by Mitchell Beaz
an imprint of Octopus Publishing Group Ltd
Carmelite House
50 Victoria Embankment
London EC4Y 0DZ
www.octopusbooks.co.uk
www.octopusbooksusa.com

Distributed in the US by
Hachette Book Group
1290 Avenue of the Americas
4th and 5th Floors
New York, NY 10104

Distributed in Canada by
Canadian Manda Group
664 Annette St.
Toronto, Ontario, Canada M6S 2C8

ISBN 978-17847-2-554-9

A CIP catalogue record for this book is available from
the British Library.

Printed and bound by CPI Group (UK) Ltd, Croydon, CR0 4YY

10 9 8 7 6 5 4 3 2 1

Publishing Director: Stephanie Jackson
Creative Director: Jonathan Christie
Senior Editor: Alex Stetter
Senior Production Manager: Peter Hunt

Versions of some of the recipes and tales in this book previously
appeared in the following publications: *City AM*: pp34, 179, 199, 200;
Esquire: p240; *GQ*: pp11-16, 193, 194; *The Independent*: pp35, 43,
44, 47, 49, 51, 57, 61, 72, 75, 88, 96, 97, 104, 113, 120, 121, 127, 131, 145,
154, 200, 201, 231, 247. All reasonable care has been taken to trace the
owners of copyright material. Anyone who may have been inadvertently
omitted is invited to write to the publishers who will be pleased to make
any necessary amendments to future printings of this publication.

Contents

Foreword
by Stephen Webster

Mark Hix – the one that got away

Japanese folklore has it that an unlucky fisherman, after many days spent in the lotus position on the riverbank with not so much as a nibble, finally lost his Japanese discipline, broke down and ate his bait, thereby inventing sushi. To my knowledge, Mark has never eaten his bait, but I do know that he has never let the lack of a catch determine whether he and his fellow fishermen enjoy a good lunch or not.

Mark absolutely loves fishing, and for him, like most fishermen, the escape from the city and the break from the daily grind are as important as what ends up in the keepnet. Despite the pastime, hobby, obsession being classified as a sport, Mark has been quoted as disagreeing with that classification. Admittedly, when he hooked and landed a sailfish weighing 40kg (88lb) off the coast of Costa Rica, the ensuing 45-minute battle between man and beast was as knackering as a 100-yard dash. On the whole, a fishing trip is more gastronomical endurance than physically exertive.

I consider myself fortunate to have accompanied Mark on several fishing excursions. On the first, I was tasked with hauling up some lobster pots that had become snagged on the seabed just off Lyme Regis. Under instruction from Mark, I held on to the rope, while he slowly motored the boat away from the lobster pot. However, my finger became lodged between the rope and the boat edge, and soon started to bleed. Seconds away from the situation going a bit 'Pete Tong', the pot shifted and the pressure subsided. As a consolation, the pot contained a lobster and not a crab. The next day, the chef at HIX Oyster & Fish House served up said lobster in a stargazey pie, complete with a sparkler in its claw, as my birthday cake.

Mark also helped me improve my fly-fishing technique in Miami, of all places, in the middle of the Art Basel Miami fair. Despite spending several hours casting our flies in and around the mangroves in an open skiff under the blistering Florida sun, we never caught a glimpse of the bonefish we were hoping for. Instead, we landed three of the strangest-looking fish imaginable, which resembled a horse's head, complete with big brown eyes. The captain informed us that these were boxfish – a less streamlined creature you couldn't imagine. Despite this, the largest one went home with us, to be served by Mark as a box brunch.

My great-grandfather was a shrimp fisherman on the Thames. The tradition of looking below the waterline for lunch stayed with my family, and my father, brother and I bonded through fishing. Between the ages of 6 and 13, fishing occupied most of my waking hours, as we compiled our own stories of rogue conger eels, Dover sole, shrimp, crabs and dustbin bags of mackerel that my brother and I couldn't give away in our neighbourhood (back then, only cats ate mackerel in Gravesend, Kent).

Mark's Fish Tales are as one would expect – unique, global, thoroughly entertaining and loosely entwined by the sport of fishing.

Introduction

Angling: it's potentially cold, it's definitely wet, it can be lonely and chances are you won't catch anything. But it's about so much more than that to me. It's become a social event that involves cooking and having a laugh and a bit of banter with the boys.

I shoot a little bit in season, which keeps me busy when the salmon and trout season finishes in autumn and winter, but, given the choice, I'd rather be on the river or out at sea. Shooting a bird above your head is instant; once you've shot it, you wait for the next one to kill. But with fishing there's a bit of a fight – sometimes a hell of a fight, depending on what you've hooked– and then there's the opportunity to release the fish or take it home for supper.

Nine reasons why you need to get into fishing or already are

Here's how I got hooked – these things bring me back to the water again and again:

1 Fishing is incredibly addictive

When I was a kid, I was really into golf, but fishing gradually started to take over, and by the time I was 16, that was that. I grew up in West Bay in Dorset, right by the seaside, so if you saw the sea bubbling – which indicated there were shoals of fish around – you just grabbed your rod and went down to the beach or the pier. My grandmother used to grill or pan-fry mackerel when they were really fresh, and she would pickle the rest. Now, I probably go fishing two or three times a month and I can't even imagine how many hours I've spent doing it, though I'd still say it's not enough.

2 Not to mention exhilarating

Take it from me: nothing beats fishing for getting the adrenaline going. I still remember a 40-kg (88-lb) sailfish I caught in Costa Rica, back in 2002 (*see* page 234). It was caught on a fly, which is very light tackle for a heavy, fast, fighting fish, and it took a good 45 minutes to reel in. I was knackered afterwards. There's definitely a bit of that primal drive of man versus beast, though as most angling is for sport, you release it afterwards. Or sometimes it gets away from you, which is frustrating. Either way, the fish gets to live to fight another day and there's still a thrill in making the connection.

3 You get to buy kit, lots and lots of kit

Shopping for fishing tackle is like being in a sweet shop. I've probably got thousands and thousands of pounds worth, but most keen fishermen do. I have around 20 or 30 rods, and thousands of flies: there are all different types depending on the time of year, the species of fish, the levels of sunlight, for example. You can even make your own flies, but thankfully I haven't got that addiction – yet – so I go to places like Farlows in London's Pall Mall, Robjent's in Stockbridge, Hampshire, or The Tackle Box, the local gear shop in Lyme Regis, Dorset, where I have a boat. I also tend to keep one set of kit in London and another one exactly the same in Dorset, so that I don't have to transport stuff about. Basically, you can never have enough.

4   Angling can be a real adventure

You can combine a holiday with a bit of angling anywhere in the world. If there's water, there's probably fish – and no, I'm not talking about the pool. I always pack travel rods and small amounts of kit in my suitcase, as you never know. Years ago I bought a Hardy smuggler fly and spinning rod, which is an eight-section rod designed to fit in your pocket, hence the word smuggler. I take it everywhere and on a short getaway it takes up next-to-no room in a small travel bag. A few months ago, for example, I took a salmon-fishing trip to Iceland. The warm weather caused snow from the surrounding mountains to melt, so the river levels rose, meaning we only caught three salmon between the six of us. But who's counting? However, while you can be a fair-weather fisherman, if you're dead serious, you need to brave the storms, which means you need more kit, and more visits to the 'sweetie shop', just in case.

5   There are different types of fishing to try

There are more varieties of angling than I could possibly list here: fishing with lures and plugs, fly, coarse, float, freshwater. You can fish on the side of a river, or in a river with your waders, at sea, even in a canal if you're a real optimist, although canals can be great spots for the pike. The type of fishing you do is usually dictated by the season, but I enjoy them all. Size doesn't necessarily matter either, because you use different weights of rod depending on the size of what you're catching. A small fish can be as rewarding as a huge one if the chase has been exciting enough.

6   You can eat for free

One of the great benefits of fishing is that you won't have to pay for your dinner, assuming you don't count what you will have forked out after spending so long in the tackle shop. The sensation of eating your catch is indescribable. In Dorset, we often eat mackerel, which are particularly plentiful, but I also have four lobster and crab pots out there. I'll pull them in at the end of a trip and they might contain as many as six lobsters or 20 or more brown crabs and the odd spider or green crab. It's not rod-and-line fishing, but it still counts. I'll often have some mates round and cook the lobsters or crabs on the grill or in a wood-fired oven, or sometimes I'll make them into a curry. You should also remember that some species should be returned to the water, so make sure you know what you've got. And don't worry if you come home with nothing – you can still go and have a steak (more of which later).

7   It's like meditation

I like fishing in a group, but I also like doing it alone (especially if you're not having much luck, so your shame's not too public). It can be calming and takes you away from the day job. I regard it as a form of meditation, and it is. Obviously, if you're catching, you have to concentrate, but if you're not, you can often find your imagination drifting off in creative directions. You'll also try to get inside the mind – or rather the stomach – of the fish. You may well know they're there, but not what they're feeding on at that particular moment. A sea bass, for example, munches on anything from a sprat to a sand eel to a small or large mackerel, so you might need to try different flies or lures, or even live bait. I fished in the New Forest recently and caught three big trout in 15 minutes, just because I randomly put on one green fly they seemed to like, but that was more luck than judgement or experience.

8   Even if you don't catch anything, it's still great fun

In 2014, five of us visited Ballyvolane House in Cork, Ireland, owned by Justin and Jenny Green (*see* page 161). We were told on arrival by our two gillies (a Scottish term that roughly means 'fishing attendant') standing in the car park that because the water was low – the opposite problem to what we often encounter— the salmon couldn't run the river to their spawning destination and were holed up in the saltwater estuary. Essentially, there were no fish. Luckily, one of my companions was armed with a cool-box full of his very fine meats (he's a butcher), including porterhouse steaks and a big old rib of beef, racks of lamb and *guanciale* (cured pork from the cheeks of a pig). I had also brought a couple of sides of my own smoked salmon and – to wash it all down – we loaded a couple of cases with red. After lunch, we all felt reinvigorated, and during a two-hour session in the early evening, I had a brief but exciting encounter with a salmon that chased my purple shrimp fly across the surface, before disappearing down the river. It was encouraging at least.

9   You never know what you're going to catch

Landing a fish successfully or not catching anything, that's all part of the fun – the not knowing bit – and even a close encounter with a fish can get the adrenaline going for the rest of the day.

Fishing has taken me all over the world, but everything I learned was close to home. Wherever you are, wherever you go, whatever you're into fishing, I hope these tales will inspire you to pick up a rod and have a go, because unless you try, you will never know. It's quite common for new anglers to catch fish on their first attempt – I've often been 'out-fished' by someone I've only just introduced to the sport, which is momentarily frustrating but soon followed by the sense of, 'Oh, I have a new fishing buddy.'

Cast of characters

Compared to my earlier experiences as a kid, when it was simply something exciting to do at weekends, after school or on holiday, fishing has become a bit of a social event for me in later life. It's always been well documented as one of the top five most popular outdoor participant sports, but I don't really regard fishing as a sport – more of a good day out with some of my like-minded friends. I'm sure they will all agree that the word 'sport' doesn't really come into our favourite outdoor activity. And, of course, the incentive, apart from a good lunch, is to rock up to the destination with our gear and catch fish.

Cooking on an open fire by a river isn't a sport either, but it is a crucial part of our social day out. We rarely talk pre-fishing about what kit and flies we're going to take, but we do discuss what the menu is and choose wines to match. Some passersby may think we're competitive, as from the outside our fishing lunches may look a bit extravagant compared to what anglers normally consume. However, because we're in the hospitality business, these are really quite normal working lunches while enjoying some banter with friends. If there are a few of us, maybe four or five, we often use the bonnet of an old Land Rover to set out our lunch – we can present different dishes on the various flat surfaces of the bonnet, creating the perfect *grande bouffe*.

A few names and characters crop up more than once throughout the book: they are mates, people I fish with on a regular basis – and those I have the most fun with, of course. These characters play a big part in *Hooked*, even if there's not a lot of hooking going on, as you will discover. Knowledge and shared fun is what fishing is all about. I'm sure they'll agree that there is always something to learn from others – and that just when you think you've learned a particular technique, something changes. Let me introduce them:

Nigel Hill is a good example of one of my experienced fishing buddies. He's a commercial multi-species fisherman whom I regard as one of the best I know with a rod in his hand – many of the Dorset locals would certainly agree and love the opportunity to fish with him. I first met Nigel when I moved to Charmouth in Dorset. I was killing an hour fishing on the promenade using a small float and rubber lure, and he came up to me and started chatting, as you would expect from a proper local in a small village. He said he lived just near the beach and started talking about fishing, so in half an hour I got to know quite a lot about him. After bumping into him every so often for a couple of years and him dropping the odd bit of fish into my restaurant, he invited me out on his boat for a spot of bass fishing on a wreck. What a day we had: 180 sea bass in commercial rod-and-line fishing terms is a damn good catch and it was non-stop from our first drift.

The following day Nigel returned to the same wreck we'd fished and caught nothing, which is why we need to respect fishermen and the price of wild fish. Nigel is always experimenting with different lures and methods, and doesn't think twice about sharing his knowledge with me. His garden shed has more kit than the local tackle shop and enough stuff to last a lifetime – but obsessive fishermen just collect fishing equipment that may or may not work in tempting fish.

Andy Kress started the same day as me at London's Le Caprice when I took the head chef job there nearly 30 years ago. We had briefly crossed paths at The Dorchester in Park Lane a few years before, and he was doing a stint with me at Le Caprice in readiness for the opening of another landmark London restaurant, The Ivy. I took him on his first mushroom forage in Epping Forest, near where we both lived at the time. He got the bug and became a much better forager than me, learning all the Latin names for the mushrooms and the best spots to find them. In return for the small amount of fungi knowledge I passed on to Andy, he bought me my first fly-fishing rod. So that's where it started really, with trips to rivers and reservoirs, and Andy showing me the various knots and types of flies.

I first met chef **Mitch Tonks** in Wales at the Abergavenny Food Festival donkey's years ago. We hit it off straightaway and seemed to have an awful lot in common. We have become great friends and do food festivals and events together. Ironically, we opened our restaurants, The Seahorse (Mitch's place in Dartmouth, Devon) and HIX Oyster & Chop House (my first place in London), within a couple of months of each other. Although Tonksy isn't exactly a fishing buddy, he's obsessed with boats and we do fishy stuff together, which makes up for it.

Now, purveyor **Peter Hannan** is most certainly the star of meat, but he's also spent years trying to work out how to get me on the Irish fish, as year after year I've travelled to Ireland in the hope of catching my first Irish salmon, and failed. His Glenarm Estate beef features heavily on our riverbank feasts and the big chunk of beef on the barbecue turns the heads of other anglers and passersby. I recently presented Peter with the Derek Cooper Lifetime Achievement Award at BBC Radio 4's Food and Farming Awards, and extremely well deserved that was. Not that Peter needs any more awards, as he cleans up every year and often doesn't enter through embarrassment.

Robin Hutson, chairman and CEO of The PIG and Lime Wood groups, is another fishing buddy. His wife Judy probably thinks we're having an affair because, as she says, he has more photos of me on his phone than of her. This book is based on our riverside feasts: these are a must. Even when it rains and conditions are 'unfishable', our lunch still goes on – well, actually, it goes on a lot longer. Robin and I have created a new level of riverbank dining, which proves that picnics don't need to be dull and that, if you are into your food, you can create something simple but special to impress your family and friends. Our riverbank dining started a few years ago with a cold pie and some cheese and pickles from the local high-end deli in Stockbridge, Hampshire. This is opposite the must-go-to 'sweetie shop', Robjent's, as we like to refer to this tackle shop, where we purchase tackle that we don't really need to help us catch fish.

Our early days of bought pies and bits has changed a lot, and lunch on the riverbank now consists of anything from a Turkish meze feast with barbecued kebabs and quails to a simply grilled cuttlefish with salsa and a salad. We've even had an Asian broth simmered on the barbecue, while I once barbecued a 75-day-aged rib of Peter Hannan's beef and simmered a sauce with fresh morels to go with it. Robin usually supplies something special from his cellar to wash it down before we get back on the river. There have, of course, been days when we've been caught in the rain on the riverbank and, consequently, our lunch has become something of a long, drawn-out affair, but still lots of fun and full of chit-chat. Although fishing is a solitary sport, your companion is crucial. Rob is the perfect partner – but not in the way Judy thinks!

Ben Weatherall has a bit of an advantage in the river as he is just over 2m (6ft 8 inches) tall and can zoom in on a swirl in the water or a fish lying on the bottom. I make an annual pilgrimage up to Ben and Silvia's estate in Dumfriesshire, Scotland, not only to try and nail a salmon or sea trout, but also to have some fun and shoot a few birds.

Oliver Rampley is a fairly recent acquaintance, but already a great friend and fishing ally – and an inspiration. He moved out of the luxury concierge business in the UK to pursue what he loves in Florence, and now has a hunting, fishing and bird-watching guide company called Altana. I visit Ollie a couple of times a year, and we share like-minded passions on both foreign and British soil.

Steve Edge is a very old friend from when I first moved to Shoreditch in London, back in the early 1990s. I would often see him walking to work, with his hand-carved stick, wearing extravagant but elegant handmade clothing and with flowing locks of blond hair, and always thought he was one of the local nutters until I was introduced to him properly in my then restaurant, the Rivington. Once engaged, to my surprise we talked fishing non-stop for about three hours over a bottle or two of good ordinary claret. Since then, we've seen each other a lot, although we rarely fish together. But we do give each other fishing-related presents and talk about our international fishing adventures when we meet up.

Essential non-fishing kit

You don't need me to tell you what kind of fishing kit to get. Although I still probably haven't quite got enough, given the importance of what goes on around the fishing, I think it's worth sharing what I've learned to carry in the back of the car.

Portable cooking systems

A portable cooking system of some sort is a must-have piece of kit for fishing adventures. There are several great, small barbecues, stoves and ovens available that won't take up much room in the boot of your car. I've collected or been given a few of these over the years (being a bit of a collectomaniac). Here are my thoughts on the different types:

Small barbecues: You can buy various small, portable barbecues. A simple lightweight Argentinian barbecue once popped up on eBay, which I couldn't resist, and I've also added a small, light, egg-shaped portable barbecue to my collection. I'll have to build a special barbecue storeroom before long to house them all!

I should also mention the dome-shaped, stainless-steel cooking system (which barbecues, smokes and grills) that lives on my boat. This is cleverly fuelled by large, circular briquettes, and is so well insulated that you can fire it up on the boat deck or on the centre of a dining table with no burns. Even when it's at full temperature, you can lift it with your hands and move it around.

22

Oh, and I almost forgot, the great travelling bucket-style barbecue that I was given as a Father's Day gift by my friend Ewan Venters. As you can see, this was the perfect, fanatical, riverside Father's Day gift.

Fold-away barbecues: I have all sorts of other small barbecues, including one that folds up to the size and thickness of a large book. I've had it for donkey's years, and it was the first sensible, space-saving barbecue I had. Most got trashed or given away to friends or admiring neighbours on the beach.

Outdoor stoves: A few years ago I bought a stove – coincidently made in my hometown of Bridport in Dorset – which conveniently uses twigs that you can gather from the woods while fishing. You feed the twigs into the base of a fire contained within a drum-like barbecue. This stove is Robin's favourite of all the barbecues, but I like to mix it up a bit and try different ones – although I think for its crudeness it may well be my favourite, too.

Wood-fired ovens: I've also got a lightweight wood-fired oven that you can pick up with one hand. You can fire it up as soon as you get to the beach or riverbank if you've got room in the car boot.

Portable grills: My most recent addition is a portable American broiler (grill), which is a fantastic bit of kit that gets to pizza-oven temperature and can caramelize the outside of your steak in a couple of minutes.

Disposable barbecues: A disposable barbecue is also pretty handy, in case you fancy a spontaneous barbecue on the beach or riverbank. You can get special frames for these, which makes them a bit more visually appealing.

Everything else

I have a kit box that contains everything you could possibly need for dining outdoors, even napkins and a corkscrew – just imagine. The kit always stays in the box, so you're not scrabbling around at the last minute putting stuff together. Here's a list of what I like to keep in my kit box:

→ Barbecue tongs and tools
→ Clean plates
→ Carving knives
→ Cutlery
→ Plastic cups/glasses
→ Seasoning
→ Condiments
→ Napkins
→ Corkscrew
→ Kitchen paper
→ Bin liners
→ Soap and water
→ Hand sanitizer

Organization is key, so, of course, there is also a cocktail shaker filled with a frozen cocktail such as a margarita. This serves two purposes: to keep the ingredients cold and to kick-start the day – unless it's a bit chilly, when a warm Shell Shot (*see* page 233) or a duck shot made with hot stock comes with us in a Thermos flask instead.

Pre-prepared cocktails can be fun to take on a fishing trip, wherever you are in the world. I've worked out that if you put water in the Thermos flask first, then pour the cocktail mix on top, you can give it a final shake or stir when it's cocktail hour and pour it. I've also tried freezing the whole flask of cocktail mix and ice cubes with the lid off so that it freezes completely (although this depends on the alcohol content of the cocktail). This works really well, and Robin and I bought two special serve flasks, which we take to the Bahamas' Andros Island (*see* page 220), or wherever we're heading.

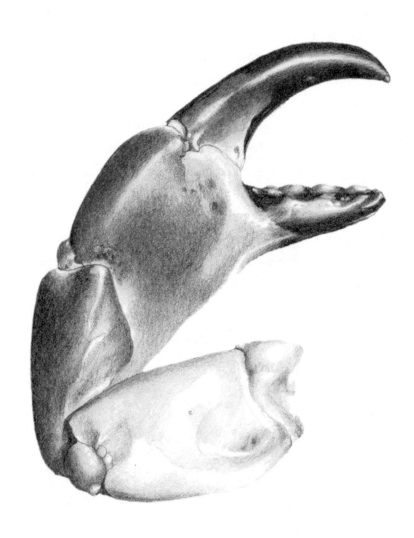

1.

Beginnings

Early experiences growing up

As a young kid growing up by the sea in West Bay, Dorset, fishing seemed a natural thing to do in my spare time. Well, for me it did, although not many at my school seemed to share the same thoughts or even think that way – except for a couple of close school friends who were my early angling and prawning buddies.

Poaching was rife among the locals, and some of my school friends, seduced into it by family and friends, would travel far to net a productive salmon and sea trout river at night when the farmers were sleeping. You would hear stories of guns and other weapons being used to field off rival poaching gangs, and I discovered when I was a bit older that the guys from Bridport had a national reputation for poaching. A successful haul of salmon or sea trout from a river would be recognized by a mention in the local newspaper, the *Bridport News*. Everyone knew the poachers and they all had nicknames. Today, I find myself having a pint or two with the ones who are still alive, openly telling interesting, funny and scary stories of what used to happen. One of them has even written a book called *Ho! Ho! Ho! A-Poaching We Will Go!*, which made the front page of the *Bridport News*!

I saw the sea on those days that I lived with my father, who had a house overlooking the bay. I would often do a detour along the promenade and around the harbour to the school bus stop, looking out for grey mullet and occasionally salmon and sea trout waiting to go up the river by the sluice gates. I had this curiosity and fascination for the mysteriousness of it all, especially while staring out to sea from the beach in both calm and angry, stormy conditions when waves would often break over the pier and promenade during winter gales.

Whatever the conditions, I found the sea rather calming and still do today. I've had a boat in the harbour in Lyme Regis, Dorset, for a few years and love hanging out with the local fishermen, talking fish and fishing just as I did as a kid. I've always found that the harbour has a lovely social element – in fact, it sometimes takes me a while to walk to my boat on the pontoon because everyone wants to chat.

What do they want to chat about, you may wonder? Well, there's Virgil, the local window cleaner, who is a great bass fisherman. He now has a commercial licence and loves to talk about new lures, reels and rods he's bought. There's Steve who has a charter boat, as well as a deli and a café on the beach, and teaches boat safety in his classroom on the Cobb. Grahame, the harbour master, and his team are always friendly, and give me the occasional friendly bollocking for driving my 4x4 a bit too far along the Cobb, or a couple of miles per hour too quickly. Harry May has the mackerel charter boat and a cab company, and often calls me about random stuff such as a new local yogurt he's tried or to warn me that the seagulls have attacked the bins outside the restaurant. A handful of characters that you may well bump into on the way to your boat, so it's always wise to set off a bit earlier to allow for chat.

Growing up, I had a fascination for fishing boats and trawlers, including their colours and shapes, and all the fishing gear hanging from their beams or on the harbour side when not in use. I knew the names of all the boats and their owners, and would sit on the harbour wall watching them load their catch into trucks on the quay to be shipped to market. When I was about six, I remember the whole of West Bay flooding with an extraordinary mix of rough seas, heavy rain and an exceptional spring tide all at once. It was terrible at the time. A lot of locals had to move out of their homes for months and businesses were disrupted. But for a kid on the clifftops, it was just incredible to see what the angry sea had done to these innocent local people and their families.

I suppose growing up on the water and being a member of the local Sea Scouts, I just took the sea and the beautiful coastline for granted. As kids we spent an awful lot of time in the water, playing junior water polo or jumping off the end of the pier, as early in the year as Easter, and having swimming races in the estuary. Sometimes we used to help out the rowing-boat hire guys on the river when they needed a break, in exchange for a free boat as and when we wanted. In fact, Carl Salter, who operated one of the two river hire boats and the trampolines in front of the tackle shop, was the guy who called me randomly one day, just before I opened HIX Oyster & Chop House in London, and asked if I wanted a restaurant in Lyme Regis overlooking the sea. I jumped on the train, got off at Axminster and grabbed a cab to Lyme Regis. It didn't take much convincing. The shell of the building that Carl had built out of reclaimed wood was perfect in every way, and we shook hands and did the deal on what was to be HIX Oyster & Fish House.

My father encouraged me to swim. Every year we would take part in the Black Buoy Race, which involved swimming half a mile out to sea to the buoy and back again, whatever the conditions. This certainly toughened you up as a swimmer because, in choppy conditions, that mile swim turned into a two-mile swim.

When I first moved to London at 18, a bit green behind the ears and as nervous as hell, I hardly ever went back to Dorset because life was busy and hectic in the hotel world, plus there were lots of parties to go to and people to meet. I used to work as much as possible and do casual work on HMS *Belfast* on the Thames and at the American ambassador's residence, Winfield House, to earn extra money for going out, as the wages were pretty poor back then for young commis chefs – and, of course, it was extra experience. But later in life, I suddenly thought: 'What a great part of the world to be brought up in. I should go back more often for some fresh air to escape the big smoke.' So, I would occasionally take friends down with me, as I was proud of my hometown.

Golf was my passion from the age of 11, as my dad got me into caddying for him when he played in club competitions and also for some of the other senior members I got to know. I used to caddie for him all the time at weekends and when he travelled to other clubs to play with the club team. He would encourage me to swing his clubs, which were way too long for me, and then bought me a set of shortened clubs when he thought the time was right – and I got addicted to the game.

On Saturday mornings and in the holidays, I used to earn a few quid caddying and working for one of the senior members, Jack White, in his plumbing supply shop, stacking pipes on the shelves and loading up his vans for deliveries. I quite liked this under-age working, probably because it installed a bit of a work ethic in me for later in life. I could work a shift in the morning and be on the golf course by lunchtime, and in the summer fish till dark in the evening, cramming as much stuff in as I could.

There was a small group of junior members and we played golf at every given opportunity. The school even gave us Thursday afternoons off to play, as they saw us as keen potential golfers. Later, when I got to 15, I became more interested in catching fish than chasing a ball around the golf course. Both kept me off the streets, I suppose, and also taught me a thing or two about etiquette, especially while playing golf with senior members and listening to the banter in the clubhouse after a game when everyone would play cards and drink beer and whisky. My dad used to buy me a weak ginger beer shandy, which I still drink to this day, as it's a great thirst quencher.

Back to fishing, though. The thrill of being on the water, hooking a fish and catching your supper, as well as the whole sustainability thing, caught my attention. My dad's friends fished for a living and had boats in the harbour. I used to stand on the harbour and watch them come in with their catch. My school friend Mark Hawker's dad Pat had a trawler and in the season would catch 'queenies'. These little queen scallops would be piled high in his boat in red net sacks and I would watch with interest as the boat came through the piers to moor up in the harbour. Mark's mum would cook the scallops and give us some to take to school in little polystyrene cups as a treat. They would be doused in vinegar and not really cleaned at all, and that memory still stays with us: standing on the edge of the playground at primary school munching away at freshly caught queenies. Maybe that's where my taste for simple luxury began – who knows. I didn't used to think anything of it because it just happened. We ate the scallops, much to the disgust of our classmates (not that I would have shared them anyway, as they tasted delicious).

Baked queenies

Serves 4–6

Today we serve queen scallops in many different ways, but I'm always reminded of my primary school childhood and snacking on them in the playground. When I was a kid, the locals and fishermen always called these little scallops queenies. In this recipe, you can use flat or curly leaf parsley for the herby crust, although I prefer the taste of the flat leaf variety.

30–40 very fresh queen scallops, opened, cleaned and left on the half-shell, or around 500g (1lb 2oz) scallops, shelled, cleaned and the half-shells reserved

For the garlic butter:

125g (4½oz) unsalted butter

2 garlic cloves, crushed

For the parsley crust:

45g (1½oz) unsalted butter

2 garlic cloves, crushed, or 2 tablespoons chopped wild garlic (ramson) leaves

2 tablespoons finely chopped parsley

45g (1½oz) fresh white breadcrumbs

Salt and pepper

To make the parsley crust, melt the butter in a saucepan and cook the garlic gently for 1 minute. Stir in the parsley and breadcrumbs, then season to taste with salt and pepper. Preheat a grill to maximum temperature. Lay the scallops, in their half-shells, on a grill tray, scatter with the parsley crust and cook under a hot grill for 3–4 minutes, or until lightly coloured. Meanwhile, make the garlic butter by melting the butter in a pan until foaming, then add the garlic, remove from the heat and spoon over the scallops.

When I was very young, my dad and his mates used to have this ritual in late autumn. I remember how they would wait on the beach in West Bay with small rowing boats and seine nets. These nets hang vertically in the water with floats at the top and weights at the bottom. The ends are then drawn together to catch the fish. They were expecting huge shoals of sprats and would stand patiently, smoking cigarettes. When they spotted the water boiling with these little fish just offshore, they would set off with the seine net between two boats and encircle the shoal to capture as many as possible. Sometimes there were half a dozen boats and 12 guys, and the fish were so close that they would be driven up on the beach of their own accord. We could pick fish up off the pebbles and pop them into fish boxes. It seemed like a cult thing to do among the locals to get a few beer vouchers from local restaurants in exchange for the fish boxes, and so enjoy a good night out or two.

Devilled sprats

Serves 4–6

Sprats are from the herring family and are the poor cousins of whitebait. They're about 6–7cm (2½–2¾ inches) long and generally need simple cooking: coated in milk and flour, then deep-fried. I like to use gluten-free self-raising flour, so they come out really crisp. To prepare the sprats for cooking, either leave the heads on or, if they're bigger, cut them off, then run your finger down their stomachs and open them into butterfly shapes. A fishmonger should be able to order and prepare them if you haven't caught any yourself.

Vegetable oil, for deep-frying

100g (3½oz) gluten-free self-raising flour

600–800g (1lb 5oz–1lb 12oz) sprats,
  prepared as on previous page

Cup of milk

Salt and cayenne pepper

Tartare sauce or lemon wedges, to serve

Preheat about 8cm (3¼ inches) of oil to a temperature of 160–180°C (325–350°F) in a large, heavy-based saucepan or an electric deep-fat fryer. Season the flour well with salt and cayenne pepper, then coat the sprats thoroughly, shaking off any excess flour. Dip the sprats briefly in the cup of milk, then back through the flour. Deep-fry in batches of 2 or 3 for 3–4 minutes, or until golden, and drain on kitchen paper before serving with tartare sauce or lemon wedges.

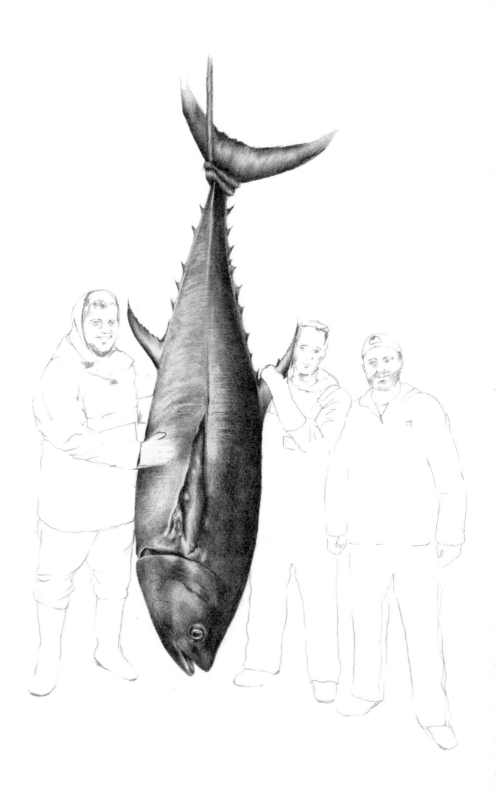

2.

South West England

Sending the kids out for fun activities and a supper contribution

Many years ago, I spent a few days over New Year at Mitch Tonks's house, overlooking the fishing port in Brixham, Devon. We were with some old friends and their kids. Mitch and I cooked up a storm on New Year's Eve with a big locally caught pollack that we lightly salted in sea water. This acts like a light brine and firms up the flesh of fish such as cod, pollack and hake, and actually adds to the flavour. If you live near the sea, it makes sense to wash your fish in sea water, as tap water does more harm than good. We poached the pollack lightly in olive oil with herbs, which was a dish that Mitch and I had during a long Parisian lunch in La Fontaine Gaillon, a restaurant in Rue de la Michodière owned by Gérard Depardieu. We recreated the most buttery mash ever (*pommes mousseline*, actually) and served it with the pollack – the mash was literally 50/50 potatoes and butter, but delicious as you can imagine (*see* the recipe for Olive oil-poached Pollack on page 43 for how to make this mash).

Mitch cooked some delicious local Devon Dexter beef chops on his bespoke, newly installed, stainless-steel, Turkish *ocakbasi* grill on his terrace overlooking the harbour. An *ocakbasi* is a pit grill used in Turkish restaurants to cook meat and fish on kebab skewers. The rest of my stay turned into a bit of a blur. Well, it was New Year.

During the day, the younger kids went crabbing off the marina pontoon. I told them to keep their catch in the bucket, as I had an idea for supper or the next day. They proudly brought back half a bucket of green crabs (or velvet or shore crabs, as they're sometimes called). I decided to make these into a crab sauce to go with a whole baked turbot we were planning to eat that night. The kids perched themselves on stools near the cooker, armed with a wooden spoon, and I took them through the process of making crab sauce. It was delicious; so much so that most of it was consumed before dinner, and we had to settle for hollandaise sauce with the turbot instead. I'm sure the kids didn't expect their crabbing expedition to turn into a cook-up with such delicious results.

So why don't we eat green crabs more, rather than regarding them as a kids' seaside pastime? Even the poor old spider crab doesn't get much of a look-in. In Spain and France, green crabs are on display in most fishmongers for using in soups and stews, but in the UK they are just regarded as a pest to fishermen because they get into their pots and eat all the bait before the brown crabs and lobsters can get to it. If they get caught up in fishing nets, they're broken out and returned to the sea dead. Shore crabs like these are part of my by-catch campaign at the moment at my Dorset seaside restaurant. I'm encouraging the fishermen to bring in these fish, dead or alive, because the soup you can make with them is delicious. They also blend up much better in the blender because their shells are softer than other types of crabs.

Olive oil-poached pollack with buttery mashed potato

Serves 4

You can make this recipe with cod as well as pollack. I've even used salmon or sea trout in the past. I've also used rapeseed oil instead of the olive oil and served the fish with a hollandaise sauce made from the cooking oil.

Thick pollack or cod fillet, about 500–600g (1lb 2oz–1lb 5oz) and 3–4cm (1¼–1½ inches) long

1 tablespoon Cornish sea salt

Enough olive oil to cover the fish

4 garlic cloves or ½ new-season garlic bulb

A few thyme sprigs

1 teaspoon fennel seeds

10 black peppercorns

For the buttery mashed potato:

1 large, floury potato (such as King Edward), peeled and roughly chopped

150g (5½oz) unsalted butter

Milk (optional)

Salt and pepper

Sprinkle the fish with the salt and leave to sit for 30 minutes. Put enough olive oil in a saucepan to cover the fish. (Use a small, tight-fitting pan, or you'll end up using too much olive oil.) Put the garlic, thyme, fennel seeds and peppercorns in the pan. Heat the oil gently and leave to infuse on a very low heat for 10 minutes (a diffuser plate works well for this).

Remove the pan from the heat, add the fish and leave somewhere warm with the lid on for 1 hour. A pan of gently simmering water with an inverted lid is ideal, as is the warming oven of an Aga. The idea is that the fish just barely cooks in the oil and becomes beautifully translucent.

To make the buttery mash, cook the potato in a saucepan of lightly salted boiling water until tender, then drain and return to the pan on a low heat for 30 seconds to dry out. Mash the potato as finely as possible, or pass it through a potato ricer. Beat in the butter with a wooden spoon and some of the cooking oil from the fish. The potato should have a thick, sauce-like consistency. If it doesn't, just beat in a little milk. Season the mashed potato with salt and pepper to taste.

Shore crab soup

Serves 4–6

You can also use brown or spider crab shells, or prawn or lobster shells, to make this soup – just make sure that the heavier shells from large brown crabs aren't blended, or it will mess up your blender blade. This soup also freezes really well, so you can keep it for a rainy-day dinner party or as a hot drink when you're fishing or shooting.

500–600g (1lb 2oz–1lb 5oz) live shore crabs (rinsed under the tap if they look muddy)

1 tablespoon vegetable oil

1 small onion, roughly chopped

1 small leek, trimmed, cleaned and roughly chopped

3 garlic cloves, roughly chopped

½ teaspoon fennel seeds

10–15 saffron threads

A few thyme sprigs

1 bay leaf

40g (1½oz) unsalted butter

2 tablespoons tomato purée

3 tablespoons plain flour

125ml (4fl oz) white wine

1.4 litres (2½ pints) hot fish stock (2 good-quality fish stock cubes dissolved in that amount of hot water is fine)

100ml (3½fl oz) double cream

Salt and freshly ground white pepper

Put the live crabs in the freezer for about 30–40 minutes, then remove them and chop into pieces. Heat the vegetable oil in a large, heavy-based saucepan and fry the crabs over a high heat, stirring every so often, for about 5 minutes, or until they begin to colour. Add the onion, leek, garlic, fennel seeds, saffron, thyme and bay leaf, and continue cooking for a further 5 minutes or so until the vegetables begin to colour. Add the butter and stir well, then add the tomato purée and flour, stir again and cook for another minute or so over a low heat. Add the white wine, then slowly add the fish stock, stirring to get rid of any lumps. Bring to the boil, season to taste with salt and pepper and simmer gently for 1 hour.

Blend the soup in a blender or strong food processor, then strain through a fine-meshed sieve. Return the soup to a clean pan, season with a little more salt and pepper, if required, and bring to the boil. To serve, add the cream, adjust the seasoning, if necessary, and stir well.

A good crab haul

I always keep a few lobster pots just off the shore in Charmouth, Dorset, during the summer months, so if the fishing fails you can be sure of at least a few crabs, with lobsters being a bonus, to satisfy your lunch or supper needs. A few years back, I had a great haul of about 20 good-sized crabs in just four pots. That evening, I was off to my friends Lloyd and Mary Lou's house for dinner, so warned them to expect an extra course, which went down a treat, as they had a few extra guests turn up.

Jeremy Lee, a fellow chef, was cooking supper, so the extra shellfish course was very welcome, and there's also no work involved, as the guests do this for you, cracking the claws with a hammer – or, as I like to do it, with a good-sized pebble from the beach. I like to serve the meat with homemade mayonnaise. If I'm tucking into a whole crab, wherever I am, I tend to scoop out the brown crabmeat and mix it with some mayonnaise and a bit of lemon and seasoning. I then spread the crab mayonnaise on some crusty buttered bread or toast, before spooning the white meat on top. I always look forward to a freshly cooked crab when heading to the coast. I enjoy sitting on my terrace at Fish House overlooking the sea with a glass of very cold Tonnix white – it's very romantic, even if I'm sitting alone. Tonnix is a seafood white wine on which Mitch Tonks and I collaborated, and we both sell it in our restaurants. We were inspired to make the wine during a wine trip to see Sophia Bergqvist at Quinta de la Rosa on the Douro, in Portugal, with our old friend and wine supplier of over 30 years. The wine's name is half Tonks and half Hix (with an extra 'n').

Hauling the pots is, of course, not always successful, but they usually yield at least enough crabs for supper, which has been one of my favourite things since I was a kid brought up on the Dorset coast. The locals would often leave buckets of crabs, as well as hares and rabbits, by my grandparents' back door. I loved eating the boiled crab with brown bread and butter, and to this day I still have a craving for this when I'm on the way to HIX Oyster & Fish House. My gran would serve the crab with salad cream back then, as I don't really remember seeing a jar of mayonnaise in the house. I suppose I didn't really know any better.

Homemade mayonnaise

Makes 350–450ml (12–16fl oz)

Why spoil a freshly cooked crab or lobster with poor-quality shop-bought mayonnaise? Years ago, I started mixing vegetable oil with olive oil when making mayonnaise for shellfish, which makes the world of difference, and combining English and Dijon mustards for a rounded flavour. If you are making tartare sauce or prawn cocktail sauce, it may not be worth making your own mayonnaise (in which case, try Delouis Fils). If you eat a lot of mayonnaise, it's worth making a batch every week and keeping it in a preserving jar in your refrigerator. Sterilize the jar first by removing the rubber ring and putting it through the dishwasher, or by boiling it in a large saucepan of water for 10 minutes.

2 egg yolks (at room temperature)

2 teaspoons white wine vinegar

1 teaspoon English mustard

2 teaspoons Dijon mustard

½ teaspoon salt

100ml (3½fl oz) olive oil mixed with 200ml (7fl oz) vegetable oil

2 tablespoons lemon juice (optional)

Freshly ground white pepper

Put the egg yolks, vinegar, mustards and salt in a stainless-steel or glass bowl, and season to taste with white pepper. (Don't use an aluminium bowl, as it will make the mayonnaise go grey.) Put the bowl on a damp cloth to stop it slipping. Use a whisk to mix everything together well, then gradually trickle the combined oils into the bowl, whisking continuously. If the mayonnaise is getting too thick, add a few drops of water and continue whisking. When the oil is all incorporated, taste, season again if necessary and add the lemon juice, if using.

Rhyming fish dishes

You don't necessarily need to catch your fish for supper, but it obviously makes a better story for your guests – unless, of course, the weather is a bit rough and you can't get your boat out, and you're gifted some fish that are tricky to catch on a rod and line. John Dory aren't really a targeted fish for anglers, as they have a delicate lip structure that doesn't necessarily hold a hook during the fight, but you do hear about the odd fish that luckily – or perhaps unluckily for the fish – gets foul hooked (or snagged) by an angler.

My fishing buddy and neighbour, Paddy Rudd, was given a box of John Dory by our commercial fisherman friend, Mushy. With my love of cooking and experimenting with Indian food, I have always liked the idea of making tandoori John Dory, not just because it rhymes perfectly, but because the shape and texture of the fish lends itself to being marinated and cooked quickly in the intense heat of a tandoor or wood-fired pizza oven, or even on a barbecue. In India, they use a fish called pomfret, which is pretty similar to John Dory but doesn't taste half as good. With this in mind, I brought some long, flat Turkish kebab skewers down from London, with which to skewer the John Dory through the mouth and out the tail so that the fish would sit nicely on the edges of my grill and could be turned easily without falling apart.

I've recently acquired a fantastic piece of British kit, a grill that's made to last out of ship steel. It has a classic retro look and is well designed, with a pulley system to lower or raise the grill bars so that you can regulate the cooking temperature accurately. You can remove the grill bars completely, so the grill doubles up as a Turkish *ocakbasi* (*see* page

41) for cooking meat and fish on kebab skewers. I bought my skewers at Ridley Road Market in Hackney, London.

I've been fascinated by Turkish *ocakbasi* restaurants since I first discovered the Mangal Ocakbasi in Arcola Street in Stoke Newington, London, near where I lived. Back then, before they expanded the tiny restaurant, one person sat behind the grill and cooked everything from the glass-fronted refrigerator cabinet, which was basically the menu. I've had Turkish grills made out of stainless steel for me in the past, copying one owned by Mitch, and successfully used them for cooking meat and fish, as well as burning aubergines to make smoky-flavoured baba ghanoush (*see* page 100 for a great recipe). They look so much more impressive and are more user-friendly than a bog-standard barbecue.

We invited some friends around and christened the Ox grill, albeit in its temporary position at Paddy's before my new house is built.

Tandoori John Dory

Serves 4

You could also make this with plaice, brill or turbot. A cucumber, coriander and mint salad is the perfect accompaniment to this dish.

1 large John Dory or 2 smaller ones, weighing about 1kg (2lb 4oz), cleaned and gutted

For the marinade:
3 tablespoons natural yogurt
2 teaspoons ground cumin
2 tablespoons lemon juice
2 teaspoons garam masala
½ teaspoon ground turmeric
1 teaspoon chilli powder
1 tablespoon finely grated fresh root ginger
3 garlic cloves, finely grated or crushed
Salt and pepper

Mix together all the ingredients for the marinade and season to taste with salt and pepper. Score the John Dory 4 or 5 times on both sides and lay in a non-reactive tray. Drench the John Dory with the marinade, cover with clingfilm and store in the refrigerator overnight. Preheat a barbecue or wood-fired oven. Skewer the John Dory and cook over the coals, without the grill rack, or in the wood-fired oven, resting the ends of the skewers on bricks or something similar. The John Dory will only take 6–7 minutes in a wood-fired oven and maybe 5 minutes each side over a barbecue. Serve the fish whole on a serving dish or board, and let your guests help themselves.

Tunny in Lyme Bay

There have been tuna in British waters for centuries. They were not really fished for sport, but back in the early 1900s, huge fish weighing over 227kg (500lb) would get caught on specially made rods and line off the East Coast off Scarborough in North Yorkshire. In those days, there was a huge herring fishery on the East Coast of England, and tunny (as it was called then) would be fished both commercially and for sport, because these huge fish would target and chase the herring. When I first heard of this, I did some research and found a couple of books dedicated to the sport: *Tunny* and *The Glory Days of the Giant Scarborough Tunny*. Lovely books, and I often buy *Tunny* online to give to my keen angling friends.

In the 1930s, an annual event started where film stars, industrialists, ladies, teenagers and military heroes would come and fish from small wooden boats called cobles, each tied on a long rope to a herring trawler, so a giant hooked fish wouldn't take the angler and the boat out into the depths of the ocean on its speedy run from its human predator and the impact of the big sharp hook. These competitive anglers would sit in their boats waiting for the tunny, dressed in tweeds and harnessed to big, thick, heavy split-cane rods with a large reel that had a huge capacity of line. The boat assistants, often young lads, would toss herring into the water to attract the fish, and the eager anglers would sit patiently with their 15-cm (6-inch), herring-baited hooks. The rods and reels weren't quite as sophisticated as today's equipment, but they certainly handled these giant predators. The books I've found have amazing photos of competitive anglers standing next to their catch suspended from winches, with the weight of the fish stuck on to the flesh. By the 1950s, this exiting period of angling had come to an end with post-war austerity, and the herring gradually disappeared in big numbers, as did the tunny from the East Coast.

Over the years, there's been the odd sighting of a bluefin tuna on the British coast and even the odd one caught by mistake. A few summers ago, I was on my boat with some friends and their kids going to West Bay, Dorset, and in the distance we saw a huge fish rocketing straight out of the water. It certainly wasn't a dolphin. We see plenty of those in Lyme Bay when we are fishing, rolling around on the surface, and we know how to identify them. This was definitely a tuna, 1.8m (6ft) or more in length, in fairly shallow water less than half a mile off the beach. It was obviously chasing up a shoal of herring or other fish, and surprising them from underneath at speed, which is why it looked like a big old missile.

Bluefin tuna are now spotted on an annual basis in Lyme Bay, and there's lots of great video footage online of huge numbers in feeding frenzies. Just recently, Mitch Tonks sent me a photo of a giant 400-kg (880-lb) bluefin that was captured by accident in fishermen's nets and will go to marine research, not the fish market for human consumption. It was like a modern-day photo of the ones in my book *Tunny*.

Bluefin tuna and other species are protected in the UK and France, and although fishing regulations in France are quite relaxed compared to those in the UK, you will most certainly end up in jail and have your boat confiscated if you are caught landing them. But who knows what the future holds. Back in the 1930s, people would pay the equivalent of £10,000 in today's money to fish for tuna off Scarborough. However, if tuna numbers rise and the fish come back to British waters, there may well be a return to the sport, but on a catch-and-release basis this time because bluefin are endangered (although given the number of fish sighted in the last few years, you would never think so). This would be fantastic for charter boat fishermen, as to date in the UK sport fishing for large fish has only applied to shark fishing. This could bring a whole new dimension to game fishing in the UK, but let's see what happens.

Imagine what a great thing that would be: anglers can't land sea bass now, but can catch and release them for sport. This rule could easily apply to tuna, too. You can't exactly hide these fish from the fish police under other fish in your cool-box, as they are bigger than an angler.

I love all species of tuna, but I haven't knowingly eaten bluefin since I saw the shocking film *The End of the Line*, which shows how Mitsubishi-owned factory ships were basically cleaning out the bluefin stocks and freezing them at -40°C (-40°F) to preserve them. Currently, the bigeye, yellowfin and albacore tunas aren't on the endangered list, but I'm always conscious that one of them could be next.

Well, the sea is certainly changing in UK waters, and just last year two swordfish were caught off Devon in fishermen's nets targeting monkfish, while four years ago an inshore net fisherman caught anchovies in his sprat nets, continued fishing the season and made several hundred thousand pounds.

I'm a keen supporter of the Blue Marine Foundation, which made Lyme Bay the first protected marine reserve in the UK. It has stopped boats trawling within 13km (8 miles) of the shore, and this has resulted in a noticeable difference in that certain species, such as cod, are staying in the bay throughout the year. The scallop beds have also recovered, with open and closed seasons in certain areas. We all need to be more aware of our oceans, so do watch *The End of the Line* if you get a chance.

Also, be mindful when buying fish. Don't always go for first-division fish, but instead try other species such as grey mullet, dabs, witch sole, gurnard and mackerel. This spreads the load a bit and puts less pressure on fish stocks. If you're unsure of what to buy, there are plenty of websites for finding out more, including the Marine Stewardship Council (MSC) and the Marine Conservation Society (MCS), as well as initiatives like Fish to Fork. These are all worth looking at before you shop, and also don't be afraid to ask your fishmonger for assistance, as it's their job to know. Annoyingly, I still see restaurants and fishmongers selling skate, which is not a sustainable species. Instead, they should be buying and selling the appropriate member of the ray family. Many fishermen, fish markets and fishmongers generalize the whole ray family and lazily call them skate, so put your fishmonger to the test.

A riverbank trout breakfast

When Robin Hutson stayed at my lodge in Charmouth, Dorset, a few years back on a pre-fishing trip, I knocked up a speedy kedgeree at his request. I'd gathered that he doesn't get kedgeree made for him that often at home and it was something he was fond of and missed. He couldn't work out how I'd prepared it so quickly while he was in the shower, as the light, fragrant, curry-sauce base is normally an hour's job – and not using curry powder, I might add. Different types of curry have different preparations of their own, as well as individual spice mixes, and a dish such as kedgeree shouldn't be too potent and fiery. Instead, it should contain the more subtle curry spices such as fennel and fenugreek, and cumin, of course, my favourite spice of all time. Well, it's all about advance preparation for unexpected guests. I always keep small batches of kedgeree sauce, along with pasta and curry sauce, in the freezer, stored flat and stacked up in freezer bags for easy defrosting.

I serve my kedgeree slightly differently than the traditional lazy kedgeree where the rice is often mixed with smoked haddock, curry powder and chopped hard-boiled eggs. I like to serve the basmati rice and the sauce binding the smoked fish as separate elements, and then put a poached egg on top. That way, you can mix it all up as much as you want or eat through the separate elements.

A pre-fishing kedgeree has become a bit of a ritual now for Robin and me, at home before we leave or on the riverbank itself. The rice can be cooked in advance and briefly reheated in a freezer bag in a pan of water on the edge of a barbecue. The sauce can be reheated in the same way, or in a pan with some chunks of trout from your previous fishing trip. If you have a smoker at home, even better, as the smoked fish gives the kedgeree a great flavour. You can smoke your trout when you get home or even on the riverbank itself in one of those portable hot smokers, then remove the fish from the bone and freeze it in usable-sized packs.

You see, barbecuing isn't always about cooking on fire for flavour: instead, light up your barbecue to make your breakfast the minute you hit the riverbank, then keep it gently stoked up for your lunch in between moving along the river. A light, tasty snack is essential to get your day going, so once you have the barbecue started, you can take advantage of the lower initial heat to fry or scramble an egg. Plus, you need a separate Calor Gas burner to get your Italian espresso machine on the boil quickly.

I was fishing on Testwood Pool, in Southampton, Hampshire, a few years back, and Robin asked if I fancied an espresso. I thought he was going to pour some boiling water on one of those sachets of instant espresso but, oh no, he pulled out this ingenious-looking little travelling espresso machine and started pumping away to get the pressure up. He then just pushed the button and out came a perfect espresso with a restaurant-quality crema on top. 'It's called a handpresso,' he said. You simply fill the little tank with boiling water, insert a coffee pod and there you go. Of course, a little nip of whisky or Somerset cider brandy sets it off nicely.

We headed down to the River Axe, which is 5km (3 miles) from my house. This is a non-documented sea trout and salmon river in fishing magazines, although I've never had much luck on it. But I've seen both species jumping and swirling in front of my eyes on many occasions, both in daylight and at night. The day before, I had an hour or so fishing up to when the sun went down and hooked a decent-sized fish. I wasn't sure if it was a salmon or sea trout. After five minutes of hooking it, the fish decided to head under a bush overhanging the water right in front of me. The adrenaline of hooking my first decent-sized fish on the Axe mellowed and, after a few tugs to try to release it, I decided to cut the line, as there was no way it was coming out with me and my fly rod attached to him.

When Robin and I rocked up at the river at the same spot, there was half a fish sitting in the grass next to the bush. An otter had obviously had more success than me and had taken advantage of my lost fish, which I identified as a salmon because of the shape of the tail – this has a more definitive point than that of a sea trout. Robin laughed, as he didn't believe there were any fish in the river and the half that the otter had kindly left us would have added up to a fairly decent-sized fish, had it not been half-eaten.

We fished enthusiastically in the same place for a bit, then moved down the river to a different spot. While we were both casting and focusing on the river, I heard a thud behind us and there was a black bull, which started running at us. The obvious thing to do was get in the river up to our knees. The bull also decided to do this, but luckily stopped with two feet in the water. We all stared at each other for a while, as water seeped over the tops of our wellies, then the bull decided to turn around and head back to his family, and we decided to quietly get out of the water and tiptoe back to the car.

Trout kedgeree

Serves 2

This kedgeree is useful for using up previously caught trout, which you can smoke and freeze for a pre-fishing breakfast, either at home or taken to the riverbank. By the river, you can heat the rice in a freezer bag in a pan of simmering water and then the curry sauce in the pan, unless you have a domestic vacuum packer, which means you can take both elements in separate bags and simmer both in the pan of water.

50g (1¾oz) basmati rice, soaked in cold water for 15 minutes and drained

Good pinch of cumin seeds

1 teaspoon black onion (nigella) seeds

1 trout (preferably smoked), weighing about 500g (1lb 2oz), filleted, boned and skinned, and chopped into roughly 2-cm (¾-inch) chunks

2 hard-boiled eggs, shelled, chopped and mixed with 1 teaspoon chopped chives

For the curry sauce:

Good knob of butter

1 medium shallot, finely chopped

1 small garlic clove, crushed

1 small chilli, finely chopped

Small piece of fresh root ginger, scraped and finely grated or chopped

¼ teaspoon ground turmeric

¼ teaspoon ground cumin

¼ teaspoon cumin seeds

½ teaspoon fennel seeds

¼ teaspoon fenugreek seeds

A few curry leaves

Pinch of saffron threads

¼ teaspoon tomato purée

100ml (3½fl oz) hot fish stock (¼ of a good-quality fish stock cube dissolved in that amount of hot water is fine)

200ml (7fl oz) double cream

Salt and pepper

First make the curry sauce. Melt the butter in a heavy-based pan and gently cook the shallot, garlic, chilli and ginger without allowing them to colour. Add all the spices and cook for a further minute to release the flavours. Add the tomato purée and fish stock, bring to the boil and allow to reduce by half. Pour in the cream and simmer again until reduced by half. Blend half the sauce in a blender, or using a stick blender, until smooth and return to the pan. Adjust the seasoning, if necessary.

Prepare the rice by rinsing it a couple times in cold water to remove any starch. Cook the rice in plenty of salted boiling water with the cumin and black onion (nigella) seeds for about 10–12 minutes, or until just cooked. Briefly drain the rice in a colander and return to the pan, off the heat and with the lid on. This allows the rice to steam-dry and gives it a nice light, fluffy texture.

To serve the kedgeree, reheat the sauce, add the trout and simmer for 2 minutes. Place the rice in bowls, spoon over the fish and sauce and scatter the hard-boiled eggs and chives over the top.

Temperley Sour

Makes 4

Lots of dishes and cocktails are often spontaneous. The Temperley Sour was the result of tidying my Dorset garden of a few handfuls of fallen crab apples. Not wanting to compost them, I made a crab apple syrup, which I then turned into a cider brandy version of the classic whisky sour. You may well not have easy access to crab apples, so to encourage you to try this, I've suggested using good-quality apple juice instead.

200ml (7fl oz) Somerset cider brandy (3 years old)

100ml (3½fl oz) Burrow Hill apple juice

60ml (4 tablespoons) Somerset Pomona

50ml (2fl oz) sugar syrup

2 egg whites

4 morello cherries in eau de vie, to garnish

Gently shake all the ingredients in a cocktail shaker and place this in a freezer overnight. You can take the cocktail shaker fishing with you in a cool-box and use it as an ice pack for your other lunch ingredients. Once the cocktail is almost defrosted and slushy, give the cocktail shaker a good shake until the cocktail goes a little foamy. Pour the cocktail into glasses with a cherry in each and ½ teaspoon of eau de vie on top.

A good breakfast in the fishing hut

For Robin Hutson and me, the excitement of getting on the river and starting to cast at a fish often takes precedence over more practical things like checking the weather forecast – we just get on with it and head off to the fishing spot. This is normally a beat on the River Test, in Brockenhurst, in the New Forest, near Robin's place, regardless of it being overcast or drizzling lightly in anticipation of the sky clearing, as we don't want to miss an opportunity of a fish.

I usually bring a simple breakfast to eat when we arrive at our spot. Sometimes it's a flask of coffee and a breakfast tart, although I occasionally push the boat out. Nothing complicated, of course, as we use the barbecue as you would your cooker at home. This means that once the heat is up you can virtually cook anything, which often involves a few mushrooms we have foraged in the area.

A few years back, I bought some little cast-iron egg skillets from a cook-shop in Chelsea Market, New York, which are perfect for our riverbank breakfasts. The toppings you can add are endless and they cook nicely on the cool edge of the barbecue, while some sourdough is toasting on the fire.

On this particular morning, Robin and I were all set and tackled up ready to go, but sadly the rain persisted. So we pulled the little barbecue under cover and cracked open a breakfast bottle from Robin's cellar while eating straight from the skillets and dunking our toasted sourdough into the duck egg yolk.

Well, we watched the odd trout rise and debated whether it was worth casting into the river, but when you can't see the fish, it's a bit pot luck. However, we always use duff river trips to brainstorm and talk shop, and so make good use of a lousy day's fishing. We kept dry and continued the banter until a couple of hours later we decided to call it a day and retire to The PIG Hotel for some warm undercover lunch.

Duck's egg Lyonnaise

Serves 4

If you can't get your hands on *guanciale*, which is an Italian cured meat prepared from pork cheeks or jowls (the name comes from the Italian word for cheek), then you can substitute chunks of pancetta or smoked bacon. Cook the *guanciale*, onion and potatoes in advance, pop them in a zip-seal bag and simply divide them between the skillets on the barbecue when you're ready to eat.

A little vegetable oil, for frying

120g (4oz) piece of *guanciale* or pancetta, cut into 1-cm (½-inch) chunks

1 medium onion, thinly sliced

6–8 medium-sized new potatoes, peeled and cut into 5-mm (¼-inch) slices

4 free-range duck eggs

Salt and pepper

Heat a little vegetable oil in a small frying pan and fry the chunks of *guanciale* for 3–4 minutes on a low heat, turning them as they cook, until they are lightly coloured. Add the onion and potatoes, and cook gently for 2–3 minutes until softened, then remove from the pan. Put the skillets over a low heat or on the edge of the barbecue. Add a little of the *guanciale* cooking fat to each skillet, then crack in the eggs, seasoning lightly with salt and pepper, and cook over a low heat for a couple of minutes, or until just cooked. Divide the cooked *guanciale*, onion and potato between the skillets and serve.

Mulled spice and all things nice

Makes 4

When there's a bit of a chill in the air on the boat or riverbank, this cider brandy version of mulled wine works a treat for warming the cockles, as it were. If you wish, you can replace some of the apple juice with cider. For me this is a much nicer option than the traditional mulled wine and a perfect fishing treat.

100ml (3½fl oz) Somerset cider brandy
(use more if you wish)

40ml (1½fl oz) honey

400ml (14fl oz) apple juice

4 tablespoons lemon juice

15g (½ oz) salted butter

To garnish:

4 orange wheels, each studded with
4 cloves

A little freshly grated nutmeg

For the spice bag:

Piece of muslin, measuring 10–12cm
(4–4½ inches)

3-cm (1¼-inch) cinnamon stick

1 star anise

4 cloves

2 green cardamom pods

2 slices of fresh root ginger

2 strips of orange rind

2 strips of lemon rind

Wrap all the ingredients for the spice bag in the piece of muslin and tie securely with a piece of string. Heat the spice bag and all the other ingredients in a saucepan, whisking regularly to melt the butter. Just bring to the boil and then remove from the heat. Remove the spice bag. Pour the cocktail into metal mugs or tempered glassware. Garnish each drink with a clove-studded orange wheel and a little grated nutmeg.

Canapés and curry
on the way to Dartmouth

Every year, my friend Steve Sweet, who has the best, most practical catamaran charter fishing boat in Lyme Regis, organizes a fishing trip to Dartmouth in Devon, and it tends to be the same crowd each year. We fish a couple of wrecks on the way there, stay overnight in a B&B and do the same on the return trip.

One particular year, we stopped off at a wreck called Harold's, halfway between Lyme Regis and Dartmouth. On most occasions, you can tell when the fish are there, as gannets will be frantically diving into the water, after whatever the fish are feeding on. The minute we did our first drift on Harold's, we hit into the bass, so I quickly called Nigel Hill – who had been telling me how poor the bass fishing had been. Well, Nigel was thrilled with the news – and why wouldn't I share that knowledge, as he always does the same for us and fishing is his livelihood. Nigel's current boat is a bit slow and only does 8–10 knots on a good day, so it took him a couple of hours to get out to us on the wreck. By that time we had caught a good 20-odd fish. He turned up while we were landing fish, with a smile on his face and a rod in his hand.

This particular trip preceded the complete bass ban for anglers, so luckily we were bagging up some decent-sized sea bass and had also caught a couple of cracking pollack, weighing over 4–5kg (9–11lb). Pollack are great eating fish when they get to that size: as good as cod. Nigel was pulling in two at a time, as he uses a method that's akin to fly-fishing with a second hook called a dropper or flyer that he puts a couple of feet away from the main lure – when the bass are feeding, they will attack anything that looks like a fish. Nigel was happy, and we were happy with a commercial cool-box full of fish as well as the extras and the pollack.

Anticipating a fish curry on the boat, I'd made a curry sauce and cooked some basmati rice the day before. Well, we certainly weren't short of bass, so that was to be the main ingredient for the curry. As usual, I dropped the fish in a bucket of sea water for a few minutes to firm up the flesh, which I've found is beneficial if I'm going to freeze down the fish fillets for a rainy winter's day.

Steve has an electric hob and microwave on his boat, in case you were wondering how I was going to cook the fish curry. I simply put the cooked basmati in freezer bags with a little butter and those went in the microwave briefly. Now, we had a slight technical hitch with the electric hob, which kept blowing a fuse. For some reason, our mate Jamie McNeil, who I had designated as my kitchen hand, kept getting an electric shock while stirring the curry and turning the pieces of fish with a metal spoon. Jamie seemed quite unperturbed by the small shocks, but sadly we didn't have a wooden spoon, which would have eased the tingles up Jamie's arm. But he was determined to get the fish cooked in the sauce for our lunch.

We eventually succeeded, and our fellow anglers enjoyed a fragrant sea bass curry with homemade flatbreads. I used the bass trim to make a ceviche with ponzu (a Japanese dipping sauce) and spooned this on to small pieces of Malaysian shrimp crackers I'd brought from home. These are the perfect vehicle for serving a ceviche – try them with my Barracuda and Pineapple Ceviche (*see* page 192).

I called Mitch Tonks at The Seahorse and told him to expect some fish on the house – in return for a fish supper, of course. When we moored up at the quay and carried the huge cool-box over the road, which two people struggled to lift, the staff looked on fearfully, but I said, 'Don't worry, I've spoken to Mitch. It's our supper and the rest is yours.' We headed back to our B&B, with a beer stop on the way, and showered up ready for our fish supper. Mitch joined us and took pleasure in telling a table of locals opposite us that there was an evening special of line-caught bass and pointed at us. This really livened up the fish banter, laughter and feeling of celebration, as a waiter presented a couple of the fish on a tray for them to choose from. They decided to take both. Another table clocked this and requested the catch of the day too, so all in all everyone was happy.

After a fantastic fry-up at the B&B the following day, we fished for flatties out of Dartmouth on a bit of shallow, sandy ground, with the hope of catching ray, turbot or, possibly, plaice – which isn't my cup of tea, but some of the boys on the boat were plaice fanatics. Unless it's a big plaice, which are quite rare, I'm not too bothered. We blanked, apart from a couple of plaice caught by the boys, but I was fishing for the bigger boys using large sand eels called lance, which we'd caught on the way out.

Sea bass curry

Serves 4–6

You can use most species of fish for a curry, as long as it's not fillets from a flaky-textured fish. Keeping the fish on the bone works to your advantage and you can go super-luxury, if you wish, by using lobster or crab. Some people may think it's a bit of a waste putting good fish in a curry, but I totally disagree because curry is the most frequently eaten dish in Britain, and fish and shellfish both lend themselves to spice. Some of the best curries I've ever eaten were made with fish and shellfish, and the giant prawn curry I had at Tayyabs in Whitechapel, London, many years ago is the one I use as a benchmark.

1 sea bass, weighing 2kg (4lb 8oz) or more, descaled and gutted

60g (2¼oz) ghee or vegetable oil

Flour, for dusting

1 teaspoon cumin seeds

1 teaspoon fenugreek seeds

1 teaspoon fennel seeds

1 teaspoon ground cumin

1 teaspoon grated turmeric root or 1 teaspoon ground turmeric

Pinch of saffron threads

Good pinch of curry leaves

1 teaspoon mustard seeds

2 medium onions, roughly chopped

5 garlic cloves, crushed

1 tablespoon grated fresh root ginger

3 small, medium-strength chillies, finely chopped

2 teaspoons tomato purée

1.3 litres (2¼ pints) hot fish stock (2 good-quality fish stock cubes dissolved in that amount of hot water is fine)

3 tablespoons chopped fresh coriander leaves

Salt and pepper

Basmati rice, to serve

Cut the head off the sea bass in a V-shape behind the fins near the gills. Remove any fins with a pair of scissors. Cut the fish into 3-cm (1¼-inch) thick steaks through the bone, then cut each steak in half through the central bone so that you end up with 2 D- shaped cuts. Season the pieces of fish to taste with salt and pepper.

Heat half the ghee or oil in a large, heavy-based pan. Lightly flour the fish, dusting off any excess, and fry over a high heat until lightly coloured. Remove the fish with a slotted spoon and put to one side. Add the rest of the ghee or oil to the pan and fry all the dry spices over a low heat for a couple of minutes, stirring occasionally, until they begin to colour. Add the onions, garlic, ginger and chillies, and continue cooking and stirring for a few minutes until they begin to soften. Add the tomato purée and stock, bring to the boil, season to taste and simmer for 45 minutes. Take a cupful of the sauce from the pan and blend it in a blender until smooth, then pour it back into the sauce. Add the pieces of fish and simmer for 8–10 minutes. Add the coriander and simmer for a further 5 minutes, re-seasoning if necessary. Serve with basmati rice.

Thirty-five miles, four wrecks and three fish

Although Nigel Hill is a bass fisherman by trade, we often fish together for other species like crab and lobster, cuttlefish and flat fish – or basically whatever is in season. He's one of the best fishermen I know along the coast and my favourite person to fish with, as he is always experimenting with new methods, tactics and lures. A day's fishing with him, whether good or bad, is a day well spent for me, as having a share in his fishing knowledge is always appreciated. And we have had some great days over the years, bagging up big numbers of bass, including 180 fish on one wreck with dolphins jumping around the boat while we were fishing.

I've learned that Nigel is very specific about lures. While we're fishing, Nigel will often check my Dexter wedge lure, a chunk of steel with sparkly holographic film on one side, which flashes as it spins in the water to imitate a sardine. Nigel constantly checks the lures in case they've lost their sparkle. He also checks the sharpness of the hooks and whether the swivels are turning correctly, so the potential for catching a fish is maximized.

Along with the great days, there are bad ones too, and we may well go to the same wreck the following day and catch nothing. That's a lot of miles in search of fish, and a lot of fuel and the deck hand to pay, so economically it doesn't always work out. That's fishing, sadly, and when you do it commercially, it's tough to make a living. Last spring I fished with Nigel on a day when he pulled 25 big commercial pots and got only eight crabs and a lobster, which is less than I sometimes get in my three pots.

We then went to four wrecks and covered 56km (35 miles) for one cod, a pollack and two pout whiting. Nigel threw the first pout whiting back, but I stopped him throwing back the second, as it would easily make three or four portions of ceviche. That's me imparting a bit of culinary knowledge in exchange for fishing knowledge. I took him for dinner afterwards at the Fish House, and had the ceviche with the pouting followed by some grilled turbot. I'd bought this from one of Nigel's friends who'd netted them while we were out. We'd negotiated over the side of the boat.

When I first met Nigel, he didn't eat fish because he was scared of the bones, but I've since weaned him on to it and now he loves it. Down at the Fish House, I'm encouraging the local fishermen to bring us what's regarded as by-catch in the trade. A good-sized fish like a pollack or pout whiting, for example, will have a good piece of flesh above the bones, which can be filleted off and skinned. We give the head and bones back to the fishermen to use as pot bait, so everyone wins. We use this type of fish for all sorts of dishes: raw in a sashimi salad, in crispy fried salads with capers and horseradish, and for fish and chips deep-fried in a dry cider and gluten-free self-raising flour so that it comes out really crisp. Even huss, or dogfish as the locals call it, which plagues anglers, makes good eating in a curry or fish stew, or barbecued.

Scrumpy-fried pouting with mushy peas

Serves 4

Although I'm obsessed with using by-catch like pouting, living as I do half on the coast and close to local fishermen, you can also use other species of fish such as cod, pollack, coley and huss, which fish and chip shops used to call rock salmon when I was a kid. This is highly misleading, as it obviously has nothing to do with salmon, nor does it taste like salmon. You can use most species to make battered fish, although I tend to stay clear of fish like turbot, as you just can't beat this simply poached and served with a hollandaise sauce.

100g (3½oz) gluten-free self-raising flour	**For the mushy peas:**
Enough dry cider or beer to make a	30g (1oz) butter
smooth batter	½ small onion, finely chopped
Vegetable oil, for deep-frying	500g (1lb 2oz) frozen peas
500g (1lb 2oz) fish fillets, such as pouting	100ml (3½fl oz) hot vegetable stock
Salt and freshly ground white pepper	A few mint sprigs, stalks removed

To make the mushy peas, heat half the butter in a saucepan and cook the onion gently until soft. Add the peas, vegetable stock and mint leaves, season to taste with salt and pepper and simmer for 10–12 minutes. Blend in a food processor until smooth. Check and correct the seasoning. Before serving, reheat the purée and stir in the remaining butter.

To make the batter for the fish, mix the flour with enough cider/beer to make a thickish batter, and then season to taste with salt and white pepper. Preheat about 8cm (3¼ inches) of oil to 160–180°C (325–350°F) in a large, heavy-based saucepan or an electric deep-fat fryer. Dip the fish in the batter and fry for 3–4 minutes, turning with a slotted spoon, or until golden. Drain the battered fish on some kitchen paper and serve with the mushy peas.

A surprise huge lobster and extravagant celebratory supper

Sometimes, you end up catching the most unexpected species by mistake – or luck in this case. I took my mate Val Warner fishing a few years back, as he had been nagging me, so I thought the best bet was to get him out with Nigel Hill on a wreck to fish for bass and cod – although Val kept banging on about getting a conger. Conger eels are horrible things to have on the deck of a boat, as they are slimy, scary (they will bite you with their razor-like needle teeth) and take hours to die, however much you bash them on the head. Well, there weren't any bass, or any fish for that matter, on this wreck – just that eerie silence, with not even a nibble, which normally means there's a big conger or two lurking around the wreck doing the same as us: fishing.

When drifting across a wreck with lures, you have to be extra careful not to start winding up the minute your weight or lure hits the bottom, or you will catch the wreck. On this occasion, I did catch the wreck for sure, then saved it, but my line was extremely heavy and deadweight. This could have been anything, from weed to a piece of the wreckage. Well, as my Dexter wedge lure got to the surface, I discovered that the catch was a beneficial one. Totally by chance, it was a huge lobster, weighing 3–4kg (6lb 8oz–9lb), which must have been living caught on the wreck for years, as it was encrusted with barnacles and tangled in fishing line. Our lucky day. Now the decision was whether to return the lobster and let it find the wreck again, or to put the semi-crippled beast out of its misery and satisfy the anglers who were empty-handed. Shamefully, I pulled the lobster in.

A little later, Val's rod – which Nigel had rigged up for conger – started twitching, as did Val. Then he struck and it was definitely something heavy, which could only be a conger. This was a big fish, maybe 15kg (33lb) or so. Val was much more excited than Nigel and I, but a big old fish on the end of your line is certainly exciting. I just hate the damn things on the boat. Well, that wasn't quite what we had set out for, but a conger and a big old lobster and no bass was what it was, along with a few insignificant fish. We kept the conger so that the boys at the restaurant could make a curry with it. A year or so previously, the local fishmonger had conger on his slab but very cleverly called it longfish, and it sold like hot cakes. So we do the same.

With a lobster that size and just the two of us dining, I thought we should have an extra-special treat to start with using the huge claws and leg meat, so I got the boys to knock up a lobster fondue. Val and I tucked in to start with, then had the tail simply grilled with some wild garlic butter made from garlic we'd gathered from the woods near the beach in Charmouth in Dorset. Surrounding diners looked on with envy, so we gave the couple closest to us a little taster, which they loved.

Lobster thermidor fondue

Serves 4–6

You could use prawns or langoustines here, or even chunks of a firm fish such as monkfish. When I was a kid, people told me that restaurants use monkfish instead of lobster, which I began to believe before realizing later in life that this was a load of bull.

1 lobster, weighing 500–600g (1lb 2oz–1lb 5oz), cooked

For the fondue sauce:

2 shallots, finely chopped

100ml (3½fl oz) hot fish stock (or ¼ of a good-quality fish stock cube dissolved in that amount of hot water is fine)

50ml (2fl oz) white wine

1 teaspoon English mustard

200ml (7fl oz) double cream

2 tablespoons grated Cheddar cheese

1 tablespoon grated Parmesan cheese

Salt and cayenne pepper

Crusty white bread, to serve

Remove the shell from the lobster's body and claws. Either use proper shellfish crackers, if you have them, or go at it hammer and tongs – just make sure the meat ends up in good, mouth-sized chunks. Don't throw away the shells; keep them in the freezer to make a bisque or sauce, or perhaps a Shell Shot (*see* page 233). Stick the pieces of lobster on to the ends of wooden or metal fondue skewers and put to one side.

Meanwhile, to make the sauce, simmer the shallots in a saucepan with the fish stock, white wine and mustard until the liquid is almost completely reduced. Add the double cream, bring to the boil and simmer again until reduced by two-thirds. Stir in the 2 cheeses until melted and season to taste with salt and cayenne pepper.

Serve the sauce in a heatproof pot on a table warmer or in your fondue set. Dip the lobster in the sauce for a minute or so until hot, and have a good time. Serve with crusty white bread to dip in the remaining sauce.

* * *

Every so often something unusual happens in the sea, and I've only really seen this a few times since growing up. All the species that appear at various times of the year show up for a reason, and not to just hang out on a beautiful coastline and among old ships that have sunk. Some summers the mackerel don't turn up in this part of the world until July and August. Occasionally, they rock up in the spring, and then just disappear. This is down to what they are feeding on, and it's the same with bass and other species. Bass are interesting and will only take a lure that replicates the fish they're feeding on, which could be mackerel, sprats, sand eels or horse mackerel. This can make the fishing tricky – a bit like fly-fishing when you match the hatch or the shrimp, for example. (Incidentally, matching the hatch means choosing a fly from your box that imitates what the fish are feeding on.)

Mackerel generally feed on whitebait, but you don't always see the whitebait in great numbers because they are tiny and always on the move, trying to keep out of the way of predators. A couple of years ago, that weird thing happened and the whitebait were so prolific that they were being driven up on to the beaches and people were filling up carrier bags for supper. I was on the pontoon where I keep my boat and literally scooping them up with a small meshed net I use for my live-bait well. The mackerel were going berserk for the whitebait and hitting their heads on the underside of the pontoon. I've never seen so many whitebait in my life – the sea was bubbling with them and I wonder what percentage was actually eaten by the mackerel.

Whitebait are the small fry of herring and sprats, and usually sold frozen and then defrosted. A couple of times as a kid, working in the kitchen at the Bridport Arms Hotel, I saw them fresh, landed by local fishermen. But to be perfectly honest, we've come to live with frozen whitebait and they still make a perfect comforting starter and snack.

I love the history of whitebait, but I'm not talking the West Country here. Historically, whitebait used to be netted extensively in the River Thames. Whitebait feasts in Greenwich, at the Trafalgar Tavern and the Ship Tavern, were popular events, frequented by politicians and important figureheads during their September season. The tradition of celebrating whitebait extended into Essex, and in 1934 the Southend Chamber of Commerce revived the Whitebait Festival, with a short service involving hymns and prayers (known as the 'Blessing of the Catch') taking place in Sands by the Sea, a restaurant in Southend-on-Sea. I've often recreated these whitebait feasts in London, serving big piles of fried whitebait down the centre of the table for people to get stuck into, followed by water souchet, which was, and for me still is, a hearty, white fish broth that utilized the larger by-catch caught in the whitebait nets. I love this use of fish on old banquet menus, as it makes perfect sense to use the whole catch – something I'm advocating more and more these days. I think back then that it was more of a case of this is all we have, so let's use it.

Whitebait

Serves 4

A lot of my school part-time job in the Bridport Arms Hotel consisted of flouring frozen whitebait for bar snacks and restaurant starters in between washing up pots, pans and plates. I would always munch on a few while serving, so got the taste for these delicious miniature fish at an early age. Whitebait is one of those fish for which there aren't any other recipes apart from deep-frying until they're crispy. In fact, they may be unique in this respect because you can't grill, steam or poach them, so crispy it is. When deep-frying, you need to ensure the oil is hot enough and get the whitebait as crisp as possible, as you don't want a soggy, unpleasant experience.

Vegetable oil, for deep-frying

100g (3½oz) gluten-free self-raising flour

Pinch of salt

Good pinch of cayenne pepper

200g (7oz) whitebait

100ml (3½fl oz) milk

Lemon wedges, to serve

Preheat about 8cm (3¼ inches) of oil to 160–180°C (325–350°F) in a large, heavy-based saucepan or an electric deep-fat fryer. Season the flour with the salt and cayenne pepper. Flour the whitebait, shaking off any excess, and dip briefly in the milk, then back in the flour. Ensure all the whitebait are well coated and shake off the excess flour again. Fry in 2 or 3 batches, depending on how many fish you're cooking, for 3–4 minutes, or until crisp, then drain on kitchen paper. Serve immediately with lemon wedges.

Serious riverbank stuff

You may well have heard of the historic elver-eating competitions in and around Frampton on Severn in Gloucestershire. Sadly, those celebrations have died out because the tiny glass eels, as they are also known, have become rare. They are back now using Spanish eels, which I have a feeling are fake, as I once bought a few cans and later realized they were a bit like skinny crab-sticks with eyes painted on. I suppose, if you're going to consume elvers by the pint in a competitive way, then the real thing is a bit of a waste because the eels 'don't touch the sides'.

The lifecycle of the glass eel is mysterious and, in fact, similar to that of the salmon. The eels begin life in the Sargasso Sea where they spawn. The larvae then make a long journey (lasting up to three years) to estuaries and rivers, floating in the currents of the Gulf Stream and developing into tiny, matchstick-sized eels. They spend their juvenile lives there, and then head back to the Sargasso Sea to spawn and begin the cycle all over again. It all sounds a bit bonkers and begs the question: why do they do this? Perhaps they have some kind of hereditary built-in navigation system like salmon, which also return to the same rivers to spawn.

Richard Cook and his father Horace have been in the elver business for some years now, and from their stories it's been a cut-throat one, too. I've been to see Richard and Horace several times, with Horace threatening to take me sea trout fishing, but sadly nothing has ever transpired. Still, my trips to Gloucestershire have always been extremely educational and eye-opening, to say the least. A few years back, I visited Richard and Horace to spend a night elver fishing on the riverbank. Well, I wasn't actually fishing, as the excursion was more about seeing the small handful of surviving elver licence holders at it down at Westbury-on-Severn. The short elver season, from mid-February to late May, was only just under way, and the elvers were few and far between. This meant the fishermen were barely earning a hundred quid a night compared to the potential thousands they would have earned years back on a good night.

For two evenings we joined Dave, a hardened elver fisherman, on his firelit tump, which is his 'patch' in elver fishermen's terms, on the Severn riverbank on one of the highest spring tides of the year. We waited until high tide, and darkness at about 9.30pm. Elvers have to be caught at night because they are negatively phototactic, which means that only a lack of light will bring them to the surface and close to the banks where they are easier to catch. Dave had a good fire ablaze, made from a couple of old wooden pallets, and also a few cans of local Gloucestershire cider for his expected guests.

The fishermen use a large, rectangular dip net with a long handle, which sits tight to the riverbank. There are regulations on the depth and width of the net: it should be 1.25m (4ft) long by 1m (3ft 3 inches) deep. After a couple of hours, Dave had only caught about 30 elvers, which equates to about 100g (3½oz). The price was high because the elvers were scarce, and the guys on the bank could get as much as £300 per kilo. At the height of the season, a good fisherman can weigh in quite a few kilos, which is a pretty good living for part-time fishing. These days, the majority of the elvers go to China, Japan and parts of Europe for breeding, including Lough Neagh in Northern Ireland, where Father Oliver Kennedy used to run the Lough Neagh Eel Cooperative Society and restock the lochs with the Cooks' elvers.

Richard then buys the eels back when they reach adult stage for smoking at the Severn & Wye Smokery in Chaxhill, Westbury-on-Severn. This final stage completes the eels' lifecycle. Isn't it mad to think that you'll pay up to £300 for a kilogram of elvers, yet you can go and buy the smoked eel at a fraction of the price! The elver station that Horace set up years ago in Chaxhill is crucial to the future of the eel. He has about 12 or so tanks for storing the elvers once they have been weighed in and exchanged for cash. In fact, the demand for the tiny eels was so high a few years ago that they bought an aeroplane to transport the things to their destination. Sadly, there is less and less demand for them, at least here in the UK – but what do you expect at that price?

We have always served elvers in the restaurants, with olive oil, garlic and a hint of chilli, in a similar way to my Spanish experiences in the Catalan region, but Horace showed me the local West Country way, which I've been hooked on ever since. I did add a little something to the local recipe, though, that Horace welcomed, especially when I told him how much we pay for it in London. That little addition was wild garlic (ramson) leaves. The season had just started, and Horace and Richard drove us up to the local woods in search of these fragrant leaves before we could have our elver feast. He also emphasized that good, fatty Gloucestershire bacon was a must – the fattier, the better so that it creates its own kind of rich, natural sauce to bind the elvers and other ingredients. I dished this up for Horace with a glass of Julian Temperley's Somerset Burrow Hill cider, which is from a different county but my all-time favourite, and the old boy was in heaven.

Elvers with Gloucestershire Old Spot bacon and wild garlic

Serves 2

There's not really an alternative for elvers if you haven't caught your own – unless you are abroad, as I was for my New Zealand adventure (*see* page 241), or if you cheat and use the imitation Spanish elvers. If needs must, you could make the same dish using tiny squid, or *chipirones*, as they are called in Spain, which you can occasionally buy frozen from fishmongers.

60g (2¼oz) fatty, streaky bacon (such as Gloucestershire Old Spot), cut into roughly 1-cm (½-inch) dice

20–30g (¾–1oz) lard, for frying

100–125g (3½–4½oz) elvers

20g (¾oz) wild garlic (ramson) leaves, torn

1 free-range duck egg yolk

Salt and pepper

Cook the bacon in a saucepan over a low heat with the lid on for 4–5 minutes, stirring occasionally and not allowing the bacon to colour. To serve, reheat the bacon with the lard in a frying pan on a medium heat, add the elvers and wild garlic and season to taste with salt and pepper. Cook for 1 minute, then remove the pan from the heat. Stir in the egg yolk and transfer immediately to a warmed serving dish.

Kids can catch

I've always advocated getting kids into fishing at an early age. Many people will wonder why. Well, the reason is: I fished from an early age and it taught me about safety and awareness, as well as how not to get seasick on boats. The best way to start kids off is to get them mackerel fishing, which can be really exciting and action-packed, even for grown-ups.

When my daughter Isla was just six, I took her out on my boat with my friend Paddy and his son Flynn, who was also six. We had heard from our friend Mushy, the commercial fisherman, that the mackerel had finally showed up in Lyme Bay and were plentiful – as a result, the wholesale price at Brixham Fish Market had dropped to just 20p a kilo from two quid. An orca whale had been spotted in the bay a couple of weeks previously and the dolphins were coming in close, which could well have been the reason for the absent mackerel, but who knows? It could also have been because of an absence of the mackerel's food. Young Isla and Flynn hadn't fished for mackerel before, so this was a perfect opportunity to teach them a bit of boat sense and also, hopefully, to catch some fish.

I fixed Isla up with the lightest, shortest rod and reel I had, and got some mackerel feather on. The mission was to catch some mackerel for the menu at the Fish House because they weren't in the bay in any number yet. We tried different spots quite close to shore, and then hit a shoal. Isla struggled to reel in her string of four mackerel, so had to have a little assistance to start with. She was keen to unhook them herself, but was rather young for that, so Paddy and I unhooked them for her. Isla insisted on picking them all up herself and then put them in the bucket in the fish hold. Most grown-ups would be scared to pick up wriggling live mackerel, but Isla was fearless and wouldn't let anyone else touch them. Then, once they were in the bucket, she was back on her rod for more.

Isla had a spark in her eye all day, and for days after she was telling everyone about her haul of mackerel for the menu at Daddy's restaurant. I hadn't even started fishing at six, so I was chuffed to bits and very proud that Isla had got stuck in and loved her first fishing boat trip. This is a great example of getting kids out and about when they are young, giving them confidence on a boat and handling fresh-out-of-the-water mackerel. I've now bought her a special lightweight, short rod and reel for her summer weekend visits to Lyme Regis.

That day, we caught about 60 or more fish, so we took them up to the Fish House. Isla handed them over to Jezza, my head chef, and said, 'For tonight's menu.' Jezza then simply grilled them as a main course and put Isla's Mackerel Ceviche on as a starter, which she ordered when we returned from a shower and change of clothes. As you can imagine, she was chuffed to see her name at the top of the menu. The ceviche arrived for us all to try, but Isla demolished the lot. She's got great taste buds, and when a new waiter offers her a kids' menu, she hands it back and says, 'Lobster please.'

I've since taken Isla razor-clam fishing on the Portland causeway beach. Well, this isn't exactly fishing but about catching the clams by surprise when the tide goes out, whereupon they disappear down a hole in the sand. Then you simply get the kids to pour salt in the hole and the clams stupidly think the tide has come back in – even though it's just gone out – and shoot back up the hole straight into the hand of a keen, smiling, six-year-old forager-fisher. I never did this as a kid, but my neighbour and old school friend Paddy Rudd often takes his kids to the coast for all sorts, including cast netting off the beach for whitebait and feeding mackerel. A cast net (often called a throw net) has been used in many countries for thousands of years to catch small fish or bait. The circular net has small weights distributed around the edge and is skilfully cast at small shoals of fish. I keep one on my boat, but haven't quite managed the technique. Anyway, the kids love the beach and the fishing, and we also encourage them to pick up as much nasty plastic as possible to help the ongoing environmental issue. This should be a school activity, I say, if you live on the coast, as it provides free food and also an insight into where the plastic that's polluting the world's oceans actually comes from.

A summer mackerel frenzy and false alarm back home in Dorset

I still fish for mackerel, as I did when I was a kid, but these days it's normally from my boat in the summer. When the fishing is a bit grim, you are more or less guaranteed to catch mackerel. When they are so plentiful, I just catch enough for supper, or I may take a bucketful or more to the restaurant, where they will go to really good use. It's always great to catch just what you need for supper and not to go too mad because, although mackerel are plentiful, it's sensible to be aware of sustainability. Fishing isn't about keeping everything you catch.

A few years back, when I started doing my Food Rocks festival in Lyme Regis, I would organize an interesting panel discussion based around topical fish chat, the ocean and sustainability. I'd invite a few like-minded people to discuss fishing and fish stocks, and basically thrash out current fishy subjects. Ironically, before the festival, the news was out in the press that mackerel were endangered, which I couldn't quite believe or understand, as I'd been out the day before and caught 100 fish in 20 minutes. Those panel conversations are usually a little heated at times, especially when I mix up the panel a bit controversially and you have people like Charles Clover, an environmental journalist and keen fly-fisherman, who made the documentary film *The End of the Line* (*see* page 52), and representatives from the Blue Marine Foundation and the Marine Stewardship Council (MSC). Also, there was my good friend Mitch Tonks, who has different views on fishing, living as he does in the fishing port of Brixham and owning fish restaurants, Nigel Bloxam of the Crab House Café in Weymouth, Dorset, and Billy Winters from Portland.

When the mackerel subject kicked off, I obviously threw in the fact that I'd caught a bucketful in no time the day before and had to stop fishing, as it was getting boring. It's interesting how heated these talks can get, especially when you have well-heeled, stubborn, old fishermen in the audience throwing swerve-ball questions at the panel. Everyone tends to walk away from those things none the wiser. Ironically, the following day we all found out that the mackerel news had been no more than a scam that had leaked out of Parliament, so that talk most certainly got 'soused'.

Until 2017, I would often go out alone, or with Nigel Hill, in search of inshore bass. When the fish are inshore, you can catch them really close in with light rods and lures like plugs. One summer, Nigel came out on my boat and we covered three wrecks about 13km (8 miles) out and caught nothing, so we went really close in to the beach in Charmouth, Dorset, where we both live. Nigel hooked into a cracking fish, and then I lost it in the landing net. He smiled, swore and said I had better get a bigger landing net, which I did immediately.

There is now a ban on fishing for bass for anglers, which has upset a few of my friends locally. We now have to target species like cod, pollack and sea bream, which are good fun, although the bass give a bit of a harder fight. But, of course, Nigel can catch his quota as long as he's fishing from his boat. I suppose the bass ban makes a bit of sense, but there are lots of arguments for and against it because commercial net fishermen can take a whole shoal in one hit, whereas anglers will pluck the bass out one at a time, which has very little impact on fish stocks.

A lovely – and I suppose slightly luxurious – thing I started doing with mackerel a few years back, on one of those occasions I'd pulled out a few easy mackerel when the bass failed me for supper, was to preserve them in olive oil and herbs in preserving jars. I had already got the wood-fired oven sparked up and invited friends round for a simple mackerel supper. When mackerel is straight out of the water, it's one of the finest fish you can eat, with its slightly unusual and oily flesh, and lends itself to all sorts of different cooking techniques. I once mistakenly bought a jar of mackerel preserved in olive oil thinking it was tuna. When I eventually got round to opening the jar, I was pleasantly surprised. It undoubtedly tasted better than most canned tuna you can buy, and had that old-fashioned sardines-on-toast taste.

I've since preserved my own mackerel on several occasions. It's so simple to do and makes a really handy snack to tuck into on some hot toast with maybe a dash of horseradish sauce or some horseradish root freshly grated on top. I've often taken a jar to the riverbank and toasted some bread on the barbecue as a nice breakfast or early evening snack.

Preserved mackerel fillets

Makes enough to fill about 7–8 small preserving jars (125ml/4fl oz each)

or 3–4 large preserving jars (250–350ml/9–12 l oz each)

This is a great way to preserve your catch and give the humble mackerel a touch of luxury. You can also use rapeseed oil in this dish and vary the flavourings. In the past, I've added chilli, cumin and fennel seeds. The jars of preserved mackerel make great little foodie gifts when given with some other homemade goodies. Bear in mind that once you've opened the jar, the fish won't keep for more than a few days.

6 large mackerel, filleted, boned
   and skinned
1½ tablespoons sea salt
½ tablespoon freshly ground white
   peppercorns

500ml (18fl oz) extra virgin olive oil
Toast or salad, to serve

Sterilize the preserving jars by removing the rubber rings and putting them through the dishwasher, or by boiling them in a large saucepan of water for 10 minutes or so. Cut each mackerel fillet into 3 or 4 pieces, season with the salt and leave to stand on a tray for 45 minutes–1 hour.

Scatter the fillets with the peppercorns and mix with about half the oil. Pack the mackerel pieces loosely in the jars, about 2cm (¾ inch) from the top, then pour in the oil so that they are covered by about 1cm (½ inch) and seal the jars. Stand the jars in a deep, wide-based saucepan (or cook them in a smaller pan in 2 or 3 batches) and cover them completely with water. Bring the water to the boil and simmer for 20 minutes for small jars and 30 minutes for large jars. Carefully remove the jars from the water and leave to cool. Store in the refrigerator for up to 3 months (unopened). Serve on toast or flaked into a salad.

A spanking-new white boat and a cuttlefish

My lovely, old, 1970 Chris Craft speedboat, which I'd looked after and restored over a period of eight years, suddenly sprang a leak. We discovered that it had a hairline crack in the hull due to being moored in a tidal harbour and bumping up and down on the muddy bottom when the tide went out. I wasn't sure whether to trash it or get it repaired. Well, she was a good-looking boat made of fibreglass and wood, but needed some serious work to get her seaworthy again.

I couldn't go a season without a boat, and Rob Perry Marine in Axminster, Dorset, persuaded me to buy a new practical boat for fishing that had a cabin, live-bait well, fish locker and lots of storage. It wasn't such a good-looker as the old Chris Craft, which I called Smokey Jo, because in its early life it had an old diesel engine that wasn't always reliable. It would sometimes fail, and on a couple of occasions it smoked, and I had to be towed in by my local friendly fishermen buddies. The new craft, which I named Hix Fix after our house cocktail, was brand new and blended in with the other practical, white fishing boats in the harbour, but felt somewhat luxurious with all the mod cons aboard.

My second trip out fishing on Hix Fix wasn't so great – I had a few little tugs, which I thought were pouting. I reeled in and, to my surprise, had a cuttlefish, which I'd never caught on a rod and line before. I was unsure whether to bring the thing on board, as their defence mechanism is to disperse their ink sac at predators or prey. We tossed a coin to decide, got the cuttlefish in the net and carefully got it on to the boat. It immediately spewed out black ink everywhere. So my spanking new white boat looked like an artist's canvas. We quickly unhooked the cuttlefish and got it in a bucket covered with a cloth so that it couldn't redecorate Hix Fix any more. You can use the ink sacs of fresh squid or cuttlefish – if the ink hasn't been dispersed all over your boat. The ink can be tricky to use, as it is often gritty, but I always keep sachets of ink in my freezer, just in case.

Cuttlefish ink spelt

Serves 4

This isn't a risotto in the true sense of the word, but a sort of British version of Spanish *arroz negro*. You can use either cuttlefish or squid for this dish. You'll need to order the little sachets of squid ink from your fishmonger in advance.

2 tablespoons rapeseed oil

200g (7oz) spelt grain, soaked in cold water for 3–4 hours, then drained

6 sachets (50g/1¾oz) squid ink (available to order from a good fishmonger)

1 litre (1¾ pints) hot fish stock (2 good-quality fish stock cubes dissolved in that amount of hot water is fine)

120g (4oz) unsalted butter

150g (5½oz) cuttlefish, cleaned and cut into roughly 1–2-cm (½–¾-inch) squares

1 tablespoon chopped hedgerow or three-cornered garlic, or garlic chives

1 tablespoon chopped parsley

1 tablespoon chopped chervil

Heat the rapeseed oil in a heavy-based saucepan, add the drained spelt and stir over a low heat for a minute or so, without allowing the spelt to colour. Add the squid ink, stir well and then slowly add the stock, a ladle at a time, ensuring all the liquid is absorbed before adding more and stirring constantly. When the spelt is tender and cooked, stir in two-thirds of the butter and add a little more stock if the risotto seems a bit too dry; the consistency should be wet, but not runny.

Meanwhile, heat the rest of the butter in a heavy-based frying pan and cook the cuttlefish on a high heat for a minute or so, then stir in all the herbs. To serve, spoon the spelt on to warmed serving plates and scatter over the cuttlefish.

Jersey turbot

I was assigned many years ago to write about the famous Jersey Royal potato, so, as is usual on my travels, I enquired politely if there would be a bit of fishing attached. There usually is, and it could be part and parcel of my story because, whatever you catch, the Jersey Royal is the perfect accompaniment.

Well, apart from learning the ins and outs of the world-famous potato – including how and where they are grown and the qualification for PDO (Protected Designation of Origin) status – on this trip to the Channel Islands, I had the pleasure of meeting renowned chef Shaun Rankin of Jersey's Bohemia restaurant. Our paths had never crossed before, we got on like a house on fire and, as is often the case, had lots of friends in common.

Shaun opted in for some fishing and called his friend David Nuth, who runs a charter boat. David reckoned our chances of catching a few bass were high. I had only come half-prepared with travel rods and had no sailing boots, so I went to a local sailing shop and treated myself to a pair of posh boots (which I still wear religiously on the boat when the sea is a bit choppy). They are certainly the most comfortable and smartest waterproof boots I've ever had.

We fished for bass for a few hours, catching live sand eels on tiny Sabiki lures, as we were fishing with live bait, but the bass didn't seem the slightest bit interested. So David moved us inshore to some sandbanks, as the bass often move in with the tide to feed on whatever they can. The fishing was still a bit grim and my bottom gear got a tad heavy, so I reeled in, thinking I had a big lump of weed on my weight.

Halfway in, the weed started to fight a bit and David said that it was probably a turbot. I had never caught a turbot before. My light bass rod did quite well and, as we got the fish to the surface, there it was: a decent-sized turbot. Like other flat fish and rays, they don't give you an awful lot of sport, but we got it onboard. It was a nice fish, about 6kg (13lb), which was exciting, but more for the eating, as it hadn't put up much of a fight.

Shaun was at the helm that night back at Bohemia and we agreed to keep the cooking simple. I remembered the egg sauce that we used to serve with simply poached turbot at The Dorchester hotel in London when I was a young chef there. Shaun replicated this with a few other turbot courses. Turbot is a bloody good eating fish and probably my favourite in the league of first-division fish. Of course, it tastes a hell of a lot better if you've landed it that afternoon.

Shaun inevitably served the fish with some simply boiled Jersey Royals tossed in butter and parsley. What a great marriage the turbot and Jerseys make. I see Shaun occasionally in London these days, as he has also opened in Mayfair, and we reminisce about the beautiful catch and fantastic dinner.

Poached turbot with egg sauce

Serves 4

Cooking this sauce brings back happy memories of my early cooking days when I was a new chef in London. It's a simple recipe and can be used for any poached fish dishes. I always recommend poaching the fish on the bone.

4 turbot steaks, on the bone, about
  200–250g (7–9oz) each

For the court-bouillon:

2 shallots, sliced

1 small carrot, thinly sliced

20 black peppercorns

1 bay leaf

1–2 tablespoons white wine

2 teaspoons sea salt

At least 500ml (18fl oz) water

For the egg sauce:

1 large shallot, finely chopped

120ml (4fl oz) dry white wine

200ml (7fl oz) hot fish stock (½ a good-
  quality fish stock cube dissolved in that
  amount of hot water is fine)

250–300ml (9–10fl oz) double cream

1 tablespoon chopped parsley

2 hard-boiled eggs, shelled and chopped

Salt and freshly ground white pepper

Put all the ingredients for the court-bouillon in a saucepan with the measured water – ensure there's enough water to cover the turbot later. Bring to the boil, simmer for a couple of minutes and then drop in the pieces of turbot. Bring back to a simmer and continue cooking for 6–7 minutes, or until the fish is just coming away from the bone. Meanwhile, to make the sauce, put the shallot in a saucepan with the wine and fish stock, and simmer until the liquid reduces down to a couple of tablespoons. Add the cream, bring to the boil and simmer until the sauce reduces by about half and has thickened. Add the parsley and season to taste with salt and white pepper. Simmer for another minute to infuse the parsley, then stir in the egg and remove from the heat. To serve, drain the turbot on some kitchen paper, then place on a serving dish. Spoon some of the carrot and shallots over the turbot, if you wish, and serve the sauce separately in a sauceboat.

3.

Hampshire

A vegetarian riverbank feast on the Itchen

The Hutson and Hix riverbank feasts usually require a big chunk of Peter Hannan's beef – say, a kilo rib or rib steak cooked over charcoal – with some serious red wine to wash it down. On this occasion, we fished for the first time on the Lower Itchen Fishery in Southhampton, Hampshire, where you will find trout, salmon and sea trout. The salmon method here is slightly odd and uses salmon nymph flies, which are heavy and not cast in the traditional way. Instead, they're sort of dragged under the bank beneath your feet. You can, of course, cast them out, but they are heavy old things, and I struggled.

We decided on this occasion to cut out the staple meat and cook up a bit of a meze with seasonal vegetables and flatbreads. Not that we had 'overcooked' the big beef scenario – we just thought we'd mix it up a bit, push the boundaries and cook some vegetables for a change. Simple enough, really, these days when we have such great British produce on our doorsteps.

Conveniently, all of Robin Hutson's PIG hotels have walled kitchen gardens, so we have some of the freshest herbs, salads and vegetables for our riverbank feasts. Robin's son Ollie, who looks after all the gardens at The PIG hotels, tends to grow things that you wouldn't ordinarily find in the supermarket or greengrocer.

On this occasion, we foraged early in the kitchen garden at the hotel in Brockenhurst in the New Forest, and filled a basket with Ollie's fantastic nurtured vegetables and herbs. We even relieved the loganberry bush of its fruits, which was just enough to go with our perfectly ripe Tunworth cheese (a British Camembert) as a dessert.

Sadly, the fishing wasn't as productive as our gardening for lunch. We covered a good mile stretch of the river without spotting many fish, but when you fish on a river that contains wild fish – as opposed to stocked fish – they tend to be elusive and get spooked very easily. So you need to tread carefully on the riverbank, and stalk the fish. Some parts of the Itchen also contain salmon and sea trout, which makes the fishing a little more interesting and exciting, as you don't quite know what you're going to spot beneath the surface.

I only managed to catch one trout just before lunch, which may be regarded as poaching because I cast at a fish that was a metre across the boundary of a stretch of water we hadn't paid to fish on, but by the time the trout took my fly, he was on our stretch. So I suppose I broke the law slightly, but I certainly wouldn't have got fined or locked up for what was a pretty good-sized fish. I returned the fish to live another day and, of course, we were going veggie that day, so no fish was allowed anyway.

Halloumi with Romero peppers and red onions

Serves 4

This is a dead-simple dish to do at a picnic. You can pre-grill the onions and peppers at home, or barbecue them at the picnic, as we did. If you can't find the long red Romero peppers, then normal ones will do, just quartered. (Romero peppers are often sold as Romano peppers.)

4 Romero peppers

2 large red onions, cut into 1-cm (½-inch) -thick slices

1–2 tablespoons pomegranate molasses

2 blocks of halloumi cheese, cut into 1-cm (½-inch) -thick slices

Vegetable or corn oil, for brushing

Greek basil (bush basil) sprigs, to serve

Grill the peppers and onions on the barbecue, turning them every so often, for about 4–5 minutes. Be careful when turning the onions that the slices don't fall apart – a fish slice or wide palette knife is best for this. Once cooked, arrange the peppers and onions on a serving dish and spoon over a little pomegranate molasses. Lightly brush the slices of cheese with oil and barbecue for 30 seconds or so on each side. Arrange the cheese on top of the peppers and onions, spoon over a little more molasses and scatter over the basil.

Tomato and coriander salad

Serves 4–6

The secret to this salsa-like salad is to chop the tomato very finely. Sumac is a spice used in Middle Eastern cookery for flavouring and seasoning, and has a slightly acidic, tangy flavour. Try seasoning kebabs and meat with it, or sprinkle it on salads and vegetables. There isn't really a substitute for sumac, so if you can't find it, just leave it out.

2 garlic cloves, preferably new season, crushed

200ml (7 fl oz) extra virgin olive oil

12 medium to large ripe tomatoes, cored and halved

2 medium onions or a bunch of spring onions, finely chopped

3–4 tablespoons coarsely chopped fresh coriander

1–2 teaspoons ground sumac

Salt and pepper

Turkish bread or focaccia, to serve

Mix the garlic and olive oil in a saucepan and infuse over a low heat for 1 minute. Chop the tomatoes as finely as you can, then put in a bowl with the garlic, oil, onions and most of the chopped coriander, and season to taste with salt and pepper. Transfer to a serving plate and scatter with the sumac and the remaining coriander. Serve with warm Turkish bread or focaccia, or as a salsa with grilled meat (if you're not going for the vegetarian option).

Blackened leeks with romesco sauce

Serves 4

In Spain's Catalan region, this dish is common in the *calçot* season. *Calçots* are like very large spring onions. In Spanish villages, they hold festivals to celebrate this winter vegetable. Young leeks are the nearest equivalent in other parts of the world, unless you overgrow your spring onions to leek size. You can't improve on leeks pulled straight from a walled kitchen garden and cooked on the barbecue within a few hours.

4 large or 8 small leeks

For the romesco sauce:

1 red pepper, cored, deseeded, skinned and finely chopped

2 garlic cloves, crushed

1 red chilli, deseeded and finely chopped

3–4 tablespoons olive oil

20g (¾oz) flaked almonds, lightly toasted

1 teaspoon tomato purée

Salt and pepper

To make the romesco sauce, gently cook the pepper, garlic and chilli in a little of the olive in a saucepan with the lid on until soft. Put in a blender with all the remaining ingredients and blend briefly until you have a coarse-textured purée, then season to taste with salt and pepper. Preheat the barbecue and grill the leeks over a medium heat, turning them as they cook, until they're black – yes, I mean black, as this is where the smoky flavour comes from. When serving, get your guests to strip away the blackened outer skin and then dip the leeks in the romesco sauce.

A Moroccan-inspired grayling day

One of my fishing buddies, Travers Nettleton, is a garden and interiors antiques dealer with a shop in Hungerford, Berkshire, which conveniently has the Rivers Kennet and Dunn more or less in the back garden. Travers, Robin Hutson, Mags Revell and myself comprised the four-man team that went to the Bahamas' Andros Island (*see* page 220) on the last visit, so a little fish on a countryside river for less combative silver fish like grayling wasn't as daunting as trying to catch super-speedy bonefish in the Caribbean. I thought I would up the game on the lunch a bit, so I decided to spark the little green egg barbecue up early on a low heat and get a slow-cooked, Moroccan-spiced shoulder of lamb on the go, which hopefully would be just cooked by the time we stopped for lunch.

I've not done an awful lot of grayling fishing, and, depending on where you are and who you're fishing with, the tactics differ somewhat. On some rivers, the grayling season continues, once the trout season finishes, up until March, so grayling is great to fish for in the winter instead of trout. The flies are quite similar to those used for trout, and Rob, our guide, used a technique involving a piece of sheep's wool about a metre from the fly. This acts as a bite-indicator, as the water in winter isn't always as crystal clear as it is in summer and is also potentially deeper.

Robin seemed to be fishing in the hot spot, right under the town bridge, and every time I glanced over at him he had a bend in his rod. We were fishing with exactly the same flies, but that's fishing. I think he had about 15 fish for the day, which was 13 more than me and the boys, but we all returned our catch for the next angler – that's good sport, especially for Robin, but who's counting? Grayling make good eating, and are also beautiful-looking, silvery fish, with a large dorsal fin that makes them especially good fighting sport.

Baba ghanoush

Serves 4–6, as a meze

You might think this is a dip, but I'm insisting that it's a salad because that's what my local Turkish restaurant calls it. They serve it more roughly chopped than the smoother version, but either way this is one one of my favourite meze dishes. Translated from the Arabic, baba ghanoush means: 'My father is spoiled like a child by my mother'. To give baba ghanoush a lovely smoky aroma and flavour, it's crucial that you roast the aubergines over a flame like a barbecue, or under a hot grill, until the skins are completely charred. I've given the blended version below, but if you are charring the aubergines on the barbecue, you can just scrape the flesh out and chop it up instead.

3 large aubergines

4 garlic cloves, unpeeled

4 tablespoons tahini

2 tablespoons natural or Greek yogurt

2 tablespoons lemon juice

Salt and pepper

To serve:

Olive oil, for drizzling

1 teaspoon ground paprika

Flatbreads or pitta bread

Preheat a barbecue or grill, and cook the aubergines until the skins are completely burned, turning them every so often. Meanwhile, grill the garlic cloves in their skins on the side of the barbecue (or just put them to one side of the grill) for 15 minutes or so, then pop them out of the skins when cool enough to handle. Remove the aubergines and leave them to cool. Cut in half and scoop out as much of the flesh as possible, scraping near the skin. Put the flesh in a food processor or blender with the garlic, tahini and yogurt, then season to taste with salt and pepper. Blend until smooth, then add the lemon juice and more seasoning, if necessary. Serve the baba ghanoush drizzled with olive oil and sprinkled with the paprika. Serve with warm flatbreads or pitta bread.

Slow-cooked Moroccan shoulder of lamb

Serves 4–6

Get the shoulder of lamb going on the barbecue with a low heat when you arrive on the riverbank, and give it a baste when you move down the river. Try serving this with some Spiced Chickpeas (*see* page 103).

1 new-season garlic bulb, chopped

1 tablespoon grated fresh root ginger

2 teaspoons cumin seeds

2 teaspoons ground cumin

1 teaspoon ground coriander

1 teaspoon ground paprika or Spanish *pimentón*

60g (2¼oz) unsalted butter, softened

2 tablespoons olive oil

1 new-season shoulder of lamb, boned

Salt and pepper

Soak a small log in water for a few hours or overnight (so the night before if you are planning to cook the lamb on a fishing trip). Preheat the barbecue, not using too much wood or charcoal, and place the log to one side of the fuel, as you want to slow-cook the lamb. In a small bowl, mix the garlic, ginger, cumin seeds, ground cumin, ground coriander, and paprika/Spanish *pimentón* with the softened butter and 1 tablespoon of the olive oil, season to taste with salt and pepper and then rub the mixture all over the lamb. Fold the lamb in half and tie securely with string. Brush the lamb with the remaining tablespoon of olive oil, place on the barbecue and cover with the barbecue lid. Turn the lamb every 30 minutes and add a little more wood or charcoal, if necessary. Cook the lamb for about 2 hours, or more if you wish, until it's tender. If the lamb is colouring too much, wrap it in foil and continue cooking.

Spiced chickpeas

Serves 4

These spicy chickpeas are the perfect accompaniment for the Slow-cooked Moroccan Shoulder of Lamb (*see* page 101).

150g (5½oz) dried chickpeas, soaked for 24 hours in plenty of cold water

1 teaspoon bicarbonate of soda

2 teaspoons salt

1 onion, finely chopped

2 garlic cloves, crushed

1 small red chilli, finely chopped

Small piece of fresh root ginger, scraped and finely chopped or grated

1 teaspoon cumin seeds

1 teaspoon ground cumin

3 tablespoons olive oil

1 teaspoon tomato purée

250ml (9fl oz) hot vegetable stock (1 good-quality vegetable stock cube dissolved in that amount of hot water is fine)

2 tablespoons chopped fresh coriander leaves

Salt and pepper

Drain and rinse the soaked chickpeas, then put them in a pressure cooker and cover with water. Add the bicarbonate of soda and salt. Secure the lid and cook for 45 minutes. If you don't have a pressure cooker, simmer the chickpeas in a saucepan for 2½ hours. Meanwhile, in a saucepan, gently cook the onion, garlic, chilli, ginger, cumin seeds and ground cumin in the olive oil for 3–4 minutes, or until soft. Add the tomato purée, cooked chickpeas and vegetable stock, bring to the boil and season to taste with salt and pepper, then simmer with the lid on for 20 minutes. Remove the lid, add the coriander and simmer for a further 2–3 minutes, or until most of the liquid has evaporated. The chickpeas can be served hot or at room temperature.

Tabbouleh

Serves 4–6

While dining on seafood on the coast near Beirut in Lebanon with my friend Sami, I learned that the amount of herbs used in a tabbouleh in various countries depends on wealth. I suppose this makes perfect sense, as I've had many a tabbouleh that has had far too much cracked bulgur wheat in it and thought, 'Cheapskates.' Make this at home before you leave for the river.

½ small onion, finely chopped (red onion or spring onions can also be used)

1 tablespoon bulgur wheat, soaked in a little hot water for 10 minutes, or dry couscous

50g (1¾oz) flat leaf parsley leaves, coarsely chopped

30g (1oz) mint leaves, coarsely chopped

2 tomatoes, skinned, deseeded and chopped

About 4 tablespoons lemon juice

1–2 tablespoons olive oil

Salt and pepper

Put all the ingredients in a bowl, season to taste with salt and pepper and mix well. Cover the bowl with clingfilm until you're ready to serve. Give the tabbouleh a good stir before serving and add a little more olive oil and an extra squeeze of lemon, to taste.

Grey mullet on the fire in the New Forest

Christchurch in the New Forest is a great spot for fly-fishing for all sorts of species, as the water is brackish, and the opportunity of hooking the unknown is an exciting prospect. I was fishing with a girlfriend, who ironically comes from the town of the same name in New Zealand, and we hired a boat with an outboard motor from the quay for the day so that we could explore the waters and, hopefully, find some fish. A small boat is ideal for this type of fishing, as you can move discreetly through the water and even out into the mouth of the estuary with lures or fly.

I was hoping to fly-fish for some sea bass, and had a take on the edge of the reeds. The bass fought pretty hard (and bass-like), but it wasn't until I got it near the boat that I realized it was, in fact, a grey mullet. As a kid, I used to fish for grey mullet in West Bay, in Dorset, hopping on and off other people's tenders as they cruised around the harbour to try and get close enough to the fish, and for some time held the club record. I wasn't into fly-fishing back then, but caught the grey mullet on my little light trout rod, which I used for mackerel off the pier, so the sport was great, as a mackerel weighs a fraction of my winning fish.

Anyhow, we stopped off in the New Forest and cooked the grey mullet on a collapsible barbecue – and it was delicious. Grey mullet caught in the sea before they head up into the freshwater rivers or estuaries taste great, and you could fool anyone they're sea bass. Ever since, we've called this fish silver mullet in the restaurants, as 'grey' isn't that appetizing. Using 'silver' on the menu gives this third-division fish something of a lift and, of course, prompts customers to ask questions.

Fish all over the world have different names. In France, for example, what we know in Britain as sea bass has three or four regional names – so it's all good.

Silver mullet with grilled courgettes, capers and olives

Serves 4

Fillet the mullet and remove the pin bones that run down the middle – or you can grill the fish whole and tackle the filleting after it's cooked. If you buy the fish, ask the fishmonger to prep it for you.

700–800g (1lb 9oz–1lb 12oz) grey mullet fillet, pin bones removed and cut into 4 portions

2 tablespoons vegetable oil, for frying (optional)

Flour, for dusting

Knob of butter (optional)

2 medium courgettes, cut lengthways into 5-mm (¼-inch) slices

1 tablespoon olive oil, for oiling (optional)

Salt and pepper

For the dressing:

20–30g (¾–1oz) capers, drained and rinsed

20 black olives, pitted and quartered

6 tablespoons extra virgin olive oil

Finely grated zest and juice of 1 lemon

Salt and pepper

To make the dressing, mix all the ingredients together and season to taste with salt and pepper. Preheat a barbecue or, if you're cooking at home, the vegetable oil in a heavy-based or nonstick frying pan. If you're barbecuing the fish whole, you can use a fish barbecue basket, which makes turning the fish easier, and there's also no compromise on flavour. Season the pieces of fish on both sides with salt and pepper to taste, and lightly dust with flour. Grill/fry the fish, skinside first, for about 3 minutes on each side. If you are frying the fish in a pan, add a knob of butter (this isn't necessary on a barbecue) and fry for another minute or so. Season the courgette slices to taste and cook on the barbecue for about 1 minute on each side. If you're cooking at home, heat a ribbed griddle pan until it's almost smoking, rub with the olive oil and cook the courgette slices. To serve, arrange the courgette slices on a plate, spoon over the dressing and lay the mullet on top.

4.

West Sussex

Bass on the fly

Robin Hutson and I have fished for sea bass a couple times on the waters at Chichester in West Sussex with Paul Hadden Wang, a great local, professional saltwater fishing guide – they aren't that common in the UK. Paul has a strict catch-and-release policy, as these types of waters are natural breeding grounds for bass, and it's all about the sport on the fly or with lures. Chichester is the perfect setting, as you don't have to go out into the sea, but can stay in the harbour and estuary, moving from spot to spot finding the bass. It's great fun when you actually see the fish rising to the surface in small shoals, and you can easily cast beyond them, bringing the lure carefully through the shoal like an injured fish and standing a good chance of hooking one.

We didn't have a very productive day. We did catch lots of small bass one after the other, which was rather annoying, but, as I said, the area is a nursery and spawning ground for sea bass, so at least our day was filled with constant excitement due to the juvenile fish. Robin eventually caught a decent-sized fish, which unfortunately swallowed the lure in haste and was beyond recovery, so this wasn't returned to the sea and we kept it for our supper. I like a supper challenge, and there were just the three of us, so I utilized every bit of the fish in a three-course, Asian-influenced supper, with a quick supermarket stop on the way home for ginger, lemon grass and fresh coriander.

Crispy sea bass and ginger broth

Serves 4

This is a great way to use some of your excess catch of bass or other fish, with chunks of crispy, deep-fried fish in a lovely, spicy broth. When I make this recipe, I usually defrost some frozen crab or lobster stock that I've previously stashed away, but you could just as easily use a convenient fish stock cube or shop-bought fresh fish stock, which both work fine with the herbs and spices.

Vegetable or corn oil, for deep-frying

150ml (¼ pint) milk

2–3 tablespoons self-raising flour

2 fillets from a medium-sized sea bass, boned and cut into 1-cm (½-inch) chunks

1 litre (1¾ pints) hot fish or shellfish stock (2 good-quality fish stock cubes dissolved in that amount of hot water is fine)

30–40g (1–1½oz) fresh root ginger, scraped and finely shredded

1 medium red chilli, thinly sliced

4 lime leaves

1 stick lemon grass, finely chopped

2 spring onions, finely shredded at an angle

Salt and pepper

Small handful of fresh coriander leaves, torn, to garnish

Preheat about 8cm (3¼ inches) of oil to 160–180°C (325–350°F) in a large, heavy-based saucepan or an electric deep-fat fryer. Have 2 bowls ready: one with the milk and the other with the flour, seasoned to taste with salt and pepper. Coat the chunks of bass in the flour, shaking off the excess, put them in the milk and then coat in the flour again. Carefully drop the chunks of bass in the hot oil and cook for about 5–6 minutes, or until really crisp, moving them around as they're cooking.

Use a slotted spoon to remove the bass from the oil and drain carefully on kitchen paper.

To make the broth, bring the fish/shellfish stock to the boil in a saucepan, add the ginger, chilli, lime leaves and lemon grass and simmer for 3–4 minutes. Remove the pan from the heat, add the spring onions and season to taste. To serve, divide the chunks of bass and coriander between 4 bowls, pour over the broth and serve.

Sea bass sashimi seaweed salad

Serves 4

Sashimi can work with most fish as long as it's dead fresh. A selection always works well visually and flavour-wise. If you're doing a mixed selection, then sliced scallops make a good addition.

150–200g (5½–7oz) very fresh skinless white fish fillet, such as sea bass, sea bream or cod

120–150ml (4–5fl oz) ponzu

30–40g (1–1½oz) marsh samphire, woody ends removed

Small handful of small, tasty salad leaves and herbs, such as coriander, mizuna, celery leaf, silver sorrel and rocket

5g (⅛oz) seaweed salad mix, soaked in cold water for 1 hour and drained

4 spring onions, finely shredded at an angle

Use a sharp knife to slice the fish as thinly as possible, then lay on a tray and spoon over half the ponzu. Toss the samphire in a bowl with the salad leaves and herbs, drained seaweed and spring onions. Spoon some of the reserved ponzu over the fish. Arrange the salad on 4 plates with the slices of fish and spoon over the remainder of the ponzu.

5.

Berkshire

A crayfish broil on the Wilderness

Every year I make a little charitable donation to an auction and the winner gets to fish with Robin Hutson and me on the Wilderness on Richard Sutton's beat on the River Kennet in Berkshire. The Wilderness is a wonderful and interesting stretch of water. In some places, there are lots of reeds and obstacles, where large pike hang out waiting for their prey, whether it's a trout, baby pike or a small duckling or bird minding their own business. I've yet to catch a pike on Richard's water, but you often hear a splash and rustling in the reeds, and know full well a pike has successfully nailed its prey.

Part of the deal is that I cook supper afterwards. This always involves a big pan of crayfish cooked in cider or beer with wild fennel gathered from the riverbank. I cook about 6–7kg (13–15lb), which John, the riverkeeper, pulls out of the river for us from crayfish traps. He even offers to pick out the big ones, which makes the eating slightly easier for the guests – not that I mind, but with the really big ones you get more meat in just one claw than in the tail of smaller ones.

We should be encouraged to eat more of these 'vermin' and do our bit for conservation, to avoid them all going off to China for processing and then buying them back in high-street sandwiches. I'm sure a lot of you have never tried them, or maybe you have tried the tubs of pasteurized tails in brine from the supermarket, but these are no match, I'm afraid.

Over the years, I've experimented with cooking crayfish to get the most flavour out of them, as they can be a bit bland compared to their sea-water cousins, prawns and lobster. I have a few Scandi friends and often throw a crayfish lunch or supper at home, which involves a lot of aquavit, as you can imagine, because the two are traditionally consumed together over there. With my friends' help, I've worked out that keeping the crays in the cooking liquid overnight gives them a much better flavour than a straight boil.

Between the six of us after the Wilderness fish, we had plenty of crays to get stuck into. This gives us a clear conscience that we are doing our bit for the river system by eradicating these pests, which eat fish eggs and destroy riverbanks. We usually follow with a few kilos of Peter Hannan's porterhouse or rib steaks and a bit of cheese. This particular annual fish is certainly more about the late lunch than the fishing, although we do normally pull out a few trout.

Freshwater crayfish with wild fennel

Serves 4–6

When I was in Finland a few years ago, I was lucky enough to arrive in prime crayfish season. At this time of year, the Finns pay crazy money for crayfish and wash it down with strong shots of aquavit. I also witnessed a crayfish broil-up by the Mississippi, with jazz band and all (*see* page 204). So why shouldn't we celebrate the culling of these tiny delicacies that are overrunning British waters? Can we convince ourselves that crayfish feasts are the way forward with a clear conscience?

1.2 litres (2 pints) beer, lager, IPA or cider

600ml (20fl oz) water

1 tablespoon fennel seeds or a handful of
　wild fennel with stalks

1 tablespoon black peppercorns

1 tablespoon sea salt

2kg (4lb 8oz) live crayfish

2 tablespoons chopped wild fennel or dill

For the fennel sauce:

100g (3½oz) good-quality mayonnaise
　(*see* page 47)

Handful of wild fennel or dill, chopped

1–2 tablespoons apple juice

Pour the beer (or whatever you're using) into a saucepan with the measured water. Add the fennel seeds/wild fennel, peppercorns and sea salt, bring to the boil and simmer for 10 minutes. Add the crayfish, bring back to the boil and simmer for a further 3 minutes. Add the chopped fennel/dill and simmer for another 2 minutes. Remove from the heat and leave to stand for 2–3 hours, or ideally overnight to impart maximum flavour, then drain the crayfish and serve hot or cold. To make the sauce, mix together the mayonnaise and chopped fennel/dill, then stir in enough apple juice to make a dip-able sauce.

Minced veal steak with green peppercorn sauce

Serves 4

Ask your butcher to include about 20–30 per cent fat in this veal mince. If he hasn't got any veal fat, then pork fat will suffice. Similarly, if you can't get hold of veal, substitute it for pork with the same fat ratio. You can buy fresh green peppercorns from some good supermarkets or Asian grocery shops. If necessary, you can use canned peppercorns.

500–600g (1lb 2oz–1lb 5oz) coarsest
    minced veal (20–30% fat)
A little vegetable or corn oil, for brushing

For the peppercorn sauce:
2 good knobs of butter
2 large or 4 small shallots, finely chopped
2 teaspoons plain flour

100ml (3½fl oz) red wine
250–300ml (9–10 fl oz) hot beef stock
    (1 good-quality beef stock cube dissolved
    in that amount of hot water is fine)
10–15g (¼–½oz) fresh or canned green
    peppercorns
2 tablespoons double cream
Sea salt and coarsely ground black pepper

Mould the minced veal into 4 even-sized patties, 2cm (¾-inch) thick, using a burger press or pastry cutter, or just your hands. Transfer the patties to a tray, cover with clingfilm and refrigerate. If you are taking the steaks on a picnic, store them between squares of greaseproof paper or clingfilm and keep in a tight-fitting storage container.

To make the sauce, melt the butter in a small, heavy-based saucepan and gently cook the shallots for 1 minute, stirring them as they cook. Stir in the flour on the heat and cook for 20 seconds or so, then gradually stir in the red wine and beef stock, to avoid lumps forming. Bring to the boil, add the peppercorns and simmer very gently for about 10–15 minutes (a simmer plate is good for this) until the sauce has thickened. Then add the double cream and simmer for another few minutes. Season to taste with sea salt and black pepper, and leave to cool. You can cover the surface of the sauce with clingfilm to stop a skin forming or put the lid on the pan.

To transport the sauce to your picnic, use a small clean saucepan or disposable foil pudding basin, which can sit on the barbecue to reheat. To serve, get the barbecue to cooking temperature (or cook under the grill if you're at home), season and lightly oil the steaks, and grill for 3–4 minutes on each side, keeping them nice and pink.

Watercress and shallot salad

Serves 4

This simple salad is the perfect accompaniment to the Minced Veal Steak with Green Peppercorn Sauce (*see* opposite), or any grilled meats come to that. If you're fishing by a river with wild watercress growing on the banks, then even better.

About 150g (5½oz) watercress, thick
   woody stalks removed and dried

2–3 shallots, thinly sliced

For the dressing:

1 tablespoon sherry vinegar

4 tablespoons walnut oil

1 teaspoon caster sugar

Sea salt

Mix all the ingredients for the dressing together in a small bowl, then season to taste with sea salt. Toss the watercress and shallots with enough dressing in another bowl, then transfer to a clean serving bowl.

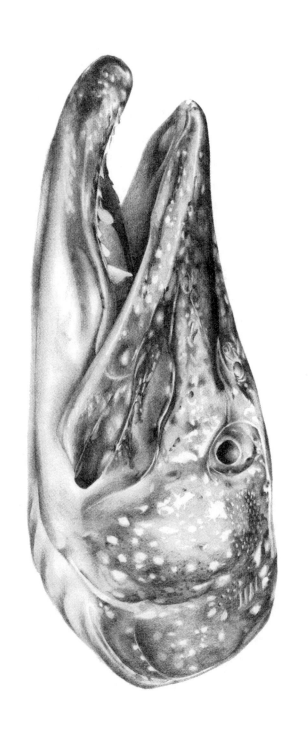

6.

East England

Hunting, fishing and foraging in Essex

When I first started as a chef at London's Le Caprice, I was asked by Jonathan Young, the then (and still) editor of *The Field* magazine, if I fancied a day's fishing, shooting, foraging and cooking for the publication in and around the Blackwater Estuary in Essex. Well, why wouldn't you, I thought, as it involved all the things I love doing and would be a great escape from London and work. The estuaries along the Essex and Suffolk coast attract wild fowl such as teal and other ducks, and are a great source of marsh samphire and other seashore goodies like sea kale, sea purslane and sea beet. If, like me, you are a hunter-gatherer, then you could really live the good life around there.

Jonathan was a perfect wild-food match and a serious hunter-gatherer. The plan for the day was to forage, hunt and fish for our supper, so in order to fit that lot in, we had to be up way before the crack of dawn. We started the day by wild-fowling at 3am, and lay in our waders and wax jackets in the marshes waiting for the sun to come up and the opportunity of a passing wild duck. As it got lighter, I realized we had been lying in beds of marsh samphire, which went on for acres and acres in the creeks off the Blackwater Estuary. After Jonathan and his son had shot a couple of mallard – I wasn't really into shooting back then – we picked enough samphire for supper and some small sea beet leaves from alongside the estuary for a salad. I wasn't sure what type of salad, as we only had three ingredients for dinner so far.

We walked a good couple of miles along the Blackwater, which is tough going in heavy chest waders, with guns and bags of wild food. Jonathan had promised wild oysters once the tide had gone out and, when we found our spot, we waded on to the estuary, where the old oyster flats would once have been hundreds of years ago. There was evidence of oyster history, of old wrecked boats that had been abandoned and dilapidated jetties for tying them up. Immediately we got on to the muddy flats, our eyes tuned into oyster shells just sitting on the mud and weed. These would have been here for years and now just grow wild for seemingly no one to harvest. We filled a couple of carrier bags, although I was conscious that this was a bit more weight to get back to the car.

Back on dry land we picked elderberries, which were the missing link to the wild duck salad dish for starters. I was hoping the fish course could be pike, and I had a great recipe up my sleeve that was given to me by the late Mauro Bregoli of the Old Manor House in Romsey, Hampshire – if one was good enough to give itself up, that is – but Jonathan was confident we would nail one. We tried hard with a fly and lures, and eventually persuaded one to move from under an overhanging tree, hooking him with a rattling baby pike imitation lure.

The great thing about autumn is the ingredients, and we finished off the day with a few handfuls of vibrant yellow chanterelles that were to be the earthy match for the pike with a light red wine sauce. We started with oysters, for which I made traditional shallot vinegar, and followed this with my mallard salad with an elderberry dressing. Dessert was simply some blackberries made into a crumble with apples from the garden and thick local cream. Now, that was an eventful day's hunting and foraging. I was bloody knackered by the end of it, and just managed to keep my eyes open to polish off Jonathan's homemade sloe gin.

Fillet of pike with crayfish sauce

Serves 4

Pike-fishing season is in autumn and winter; most rivers and some lakes allow you to fish for pike all year round. If you can't get hold of pike, try your fishmonger – or replace it with turbot, brill or its cousin, the zander (pike perch) instead. *Quenelles de brochet sauce Nantua* is a classic French dish in which both main ingredients come from the river. The key is to begin by preparing the pike, which will be double-cooked in the final stage. Crayfish make a delicious sauce, similar to a lobster or shellfish sauce.

4 pike fillets (about 160–180g/5¾–6½oz in total), steamed and boned (see below for method)

16–20 crayfish (keep the shells for the sauce)

Olive oil and a small knob of butter (if frying) or 2 tablespoons olive oil (if roasting), to double-cook the pike fillets

Salt and freshly ground white pepper

For the crayfish sauce:

16–20 crayfish shells (reserved from above)

4 shallots, roughly chopped

1 garlic clove, chopped

A little vegetable oil, for frying

Good knob of butter, for frying

1 dessertspoon plain flour

Good pinch of saffron threads

A few tarragon sprigs

2 teaspoons tomato purée

4 tablespoons white wine

200ml (7fl oz) hot fish stock (1 good-quality fish stock cube dissolved in that amount of hot water is fine)

350ml (12fl oz) double cream

Salt and freshly ground white pepper

To cook the pike fillets, season to taste with salt and white pepper, then steam for about 10 minutes. If you don't have a steamer, poach the fillets by laying them in a roasting tray filled with about 2cm (¾ inch) of hot water, cover with foil and cook in a moderate oven for 15 minutes. The steaming/poaching causes the flesh to shrink a little, leaving the bones protruding, so you can pull them out with a pair of long-nosed pliers or tweezers. There are a lot of bones, so be patient – it's worth it. The fish can then be pan-fried in olive oil and butter, roasted in the oven with some olive oil or even resteamed. Note: Because pike flesh is very firm, it will withstand this double-cooking and you can enjoy the flavour of pike as it is, rather than minced up and mixed with cream and eggs, for example (*see* page 131).

Cook the crayfish in simmering salted water for 7 minutes and then plunge them into cold water. Remove the meat from the shells and the claws (if these are big enough). Break the shells up a little with a heavy knife and set aside to make the *sauce Nantua*.

To make the sauce, fry the reserved crayfish shells, shallots and garlic in the vegetable oil in a heavy-based saucepan over a medium heat for about 6–7 minutes, or until lightly coloured. Add the butter and flour, and stir well into the shells. Add the saffron, tarragon and tomato purée, and stir well. Gradually stir in the white wine and fish stock, and bring to the boil. Simmer for about 10 minutes until the sauce reduces by about half, then add the cream. Season lightly with salt and white pepper, bring to the boil again and simmer gently for about 30 minutes, or until the sauce reduces by half and has a thick consistency.

Strain the sauce through a colander into a bowl, stirring the shells with a spoon to ensure all the sauce goes through. Remove about 10 per cent of the shells – roughly half a cup – and blend them with the strained sauce in a blender. Strain the sauce again, this time through a fine-meshed sieve. Cook the pike fillets for a second time, either by frying in olive oil for 2–3 minutes on each side, then adding a small knob of butter and continuing to fry until they are lightly browned, or by preheating the oven to 200°C (400°F), Gas Mark 6, heating a couple of tablespoons of olive oil in a roasting pan and roasting the fillets for 10–12 minutes, or until they are lightly coloured.

Meanwhile, simmer the sauce until it has a coating consistency (if it doesn't already) and then drop in the crayfish meat for about 1 minute to reheat. To serve, spoon the crayfish and sauce over the pike fillets.

Suffolk: PPP and another predator pike

When the trout season finishes, that's not the end of our fishing adventures. The main predator in many British rivers is the prehistoric-looking pike. It's a beautiful, but scary-looking looking, fish in my opinion. Pike need to be culled, as they tend to eat anything that moves and occupies a river, lake or canal. They obviously have to survive, like all species, but can reach over 20kg (44lb) and will eat other pike, as well as frogs and baby ducks, to satisfy their appetite. Many waters encourage anglers to target pike in order to keep the stocks down, but it's important to return the big pike because they play an important role in the ecology by controlling the stocks of small jack pike – yes, they even eat their own siblings.

I probably have a couple of good pike fishes a year. A memorable one was fishing up at my friend Hugh Crossley's at Somerleyton Hall, in Suffolk. Hugh has a beautiful, narrow lake called Fritton Lake, 3km

(2 miles) long, with its own pub called the Fritton Arms. I sensed a history of pike fishing there, especially when I went through his late father's gun room and found some very old Hardy wire traces in their original waxed paper wrappers, probably from the early 1900s, and big, old, antiquated spinners that would only be suitable for pike.

On this particular trip, we had been shooting pheasants and partridge on Hugh's estate, and on the way to the lodge for a proper shooting lunch, I stumbled across a big patch of mushrooms called penny buns or ceps. They are also known as porcini in Italy. Supper the following night was certainly coming together and the only thing missing was the fish course.

The river- and game-keeper, who was to take me out in his little boat on the lake the following morning, explained that no one really fishes for pike on the lake any more. This made the trip an exciting prospect, as Hugh's father's old pike-fishing kit, which I'd stumbled across, and the Pike Inn were clues to the pike history on Fritton Lake. I obviously had to do my upmost to pull a pike or two out of the lake, so I set off after breakfast. Within a few hours I had a couple of smallish-sized fish, but still plenty to feed the ten of us for supper. With the birds in the bag, a couple of pike in the net and a bagful of porcini, I set to work on supper for our guests. This consisted of a porcini risotto and a partridge salad with some wild herbs and weeds, which I also foraged by the lakeside, and roast pike.

Not only are pike great fun to catch, but prepared in the right way they're also delicious to eat, contrary to most people's opinion, due to their unusual bone structure, which is unlike most other common species of fish. They can be a pain to prepare if you don't have the know-how, because the Y-shaped bone structure and the firm flesh make them extremely tricky to bone once they are filleted. This is why most recipes that use pike are made into a mousseline, which involves mincing and processing, plus adding egg whites and cream, which can be an extremely long-winded process. I won't put you through the pain of making a mousseline, but I will share a top tip that was given to me many years ago by Mauro Bregoli who owned the Old Manor House in Romsey, Hampshire. He was a hunter-gatherer but, sadly, sold the business, which is a shame, as it was always one of those great restaurants that are fun to visit. Mauro would always pass on some useful culinary secrets.

Now, if you have stalked and managed to hook and land your pike after a good fight, then you had better put it to good use. Mauro told me that local fishermen used to bring him pike, which he would double-cook as in the recipe for Fillet of Pike with crayfish sauce (*see* page 127). He kept the fillets in the refrigerator in olive oil so that they were ready to go when a customer ordered one. Because the flesh of the pike is firm, as you can imagine just by taking one look at the beast, it will take a double-cooking, and at home you can actually freeze it in freezer bags in a little oil.

Raw shaved penny buns with Berkswell

Serves 4

Occasionally, a fishing trip coincides with a flush of penny bun mushrooms, aka ceps or porcini (or *Boletus edulis* to give them their botanical name). When this happens, you don't even need to cook the mushrooms, but just shave them raw straight on to the plate. If you can't get hold of Berkswell cheese, then just use Parmesan or pecorino instead. This dish makes a great starter.

250g (9oz) firm penny buns (ideally straight out of the ground), trimmed and very thinly sliced

5–6 tablespoons rapeseed oil

About 4 tablespoons lemon juice

Salt and pepper

To serve:

Handful of small salad leaves, such as land cress and rocket

85–100g (3–3½oz) Berkswell cheese

Put the mushrooms on a baking tray, season to taste with salt and pepper and pour over the oil and lemon juice. Mix well, keeping the mushrooms intact, and then leave to marinate for 15 minutes, turning occasionally. To serve, arrange the salad leaves on the plates with the mushrooms and pour over any remaining marinating juices. If the mushrooms have already absorbed all the oil and lemon, just pour a little extra over. Use a sharp knife or vegetable peeler to shave the Berkswell cheese as thinly as possible, then scatter over the salad.

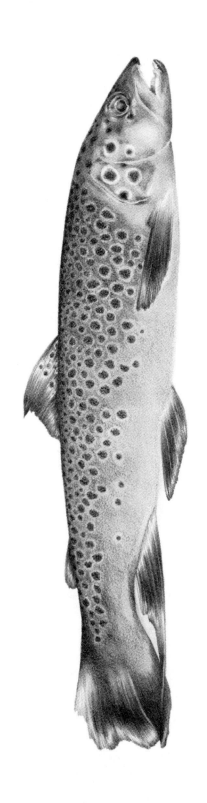

7.

Derbyshire

Truite au bleu on the Derbyshire Wye

A couple of decades ago, I was invited to fish the River Wye in Derbyshire up at Lord and Lady Edward Manners' Haddon Hall by an old friend, Adrian Houston. A handful of like-minded industry foodies, as well as fishing buddies and enthusiasts, were also invited, so it was to be a fun couple of days. It's a beautiful bit of water, running through the centre of the town, and has large rainbow trout, which are always good sport for trout fishermen. These rainbows were released into a lake near the River Wye in the early 1900s, just upstream from Bakewell. They consequently escaped into the Wye and bred successfully, which doesn't normally happen in British rivers. So this was a big bonus for anglers using dry flies on the Haddon Estate.

The fish were on the minute we started casting our dry flies into the river. Over breakfast I had suggested having lunch on the riverbank and serving *truite au bleu* using the first few fish we landed. Chef Raymond Blanc's eyes lit up with his cheeky smile. What a great day's fishing we had in such a special setting on the estate. Even those new to fly-fishing, including myself, caught fish before lunch, and at one point, looking around at our party, everyone's fly rod had a good old bend in it and there were plenty of smiling faces.

You never really see *truite au bleu* on menus any more. It's an old-fashioned way to cook fresh-out-of-the-water trout in a court-bouillon (which is a quickly cooked broth), so that the skin of the fish turns a translucent blue when it is poached. It would have been a regular dish on the menus of fancy hotel restaurants in the 1950s and '60s, where the fish would have been kept alive in tanks until ordered and then prepared at the table. Sadly, the dish has disappeared, except when I go fishing, since Robin Hutson and I occasionally cook one as a pre-lunch snack in my old stainless-steel fish kettle and eat it with a bit of bread toasted on the barbecue or new potatoes cooked in with the trout.

We tend to return our trout unless we are cooking this dish, and Robin always reminisces about the time when he was working at London's Savoy hotel and was at a customer's table presenting and filleting *truite au bleu*. As he got his knife into the fish, he realized that it was completely raw, and had to apologize and return it to the kitchen – where he got abuse from the chefs.

Truite au bleu

Serves 2

Take an old saucepan or fish kettle to the riverbank for this, which you don't mind going on the barbecue. Or there may be a posh fishing hut with a cooker if you're lucky.

2 tablespoons sea salt	1 bay leaf
150ml (¼ pint) white wine or cider vinegar	2 medium-sized trout or 1 larger one,
10–15 black peppercorns	gutted
1 teaspoon fennel seeds	

Bring enough water to the boil to cover the trout, add the salt, vinegar, peppercorns, fennel seeds and bay leaf and simmer for 5 minutes. Carefully place the trout in the simmering water and remove the pan from the heat. Smaller fish will cook through if you leave them in the water for 10 minutes. If you've caught a large fish, just simmer gently for a few minutes before removing the pan from the heat. To serve, remove the trout from the cooking liquid with a fish slice or similar on to a serving dish.

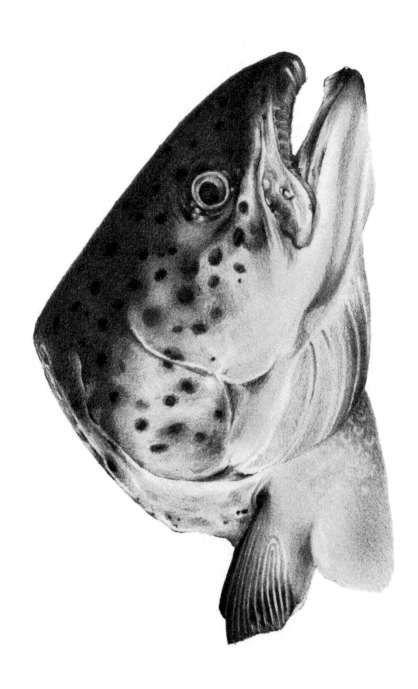

8.

London

Fishy bits

I never really got exposed to curry till I moved to London. The curry house in Bridport, Dorset, hadn't yet opened when I moved away, and back then it was a bit of a novelty to have an Indian and a Chinese in the town. Like a lot of other people, I became addicted, but the addiction was not so much about the quality and aromatic spices as that hit of whatever it was after a few beers late at night.

When I was 21, I worked at The Dorchester in London, learning my trade. We had a lovable bunch of Bangladeshi kitchen porters there who made their own staff food and this was always a curry of some description. Sometimes it was a simple white cabbage or cauliflower curry, or we would order them in some neck of lamb or chicken legs, but my favourite of all was the fish curry. Now, I'm not talking nice chunks of fish here – they would turn their noses up at Dover sole and sea bass – I'm talking bits we would use for fish stock.

What I discovered back then was that there's an awful lot of delicious gelatinous meat left on the head and collar behind the gills of some of the larger species of fish, such as cod, turbot and halibut. The kitchen porters would dissect the head, leaving the meaty bits on the bone. Because the flesh on the cheeks and collar is quite meaty, it stands up to a bit of rapid curry cooking and doesn't disintegrate in the same way as a fillet.

We took special care of the porters because we enjoyed the curry as much as they did, and used to muscle in on their staff food. We made sure the spice cupboard had everything they needed and that there was always a stash of fresh coriander. When we prepared the fish that came in for the menu, we always put something in a drawer in the fish refrigerator labelled 'Ali'. We regarded Ali as the head porter, as he had a nice smile, a bit of a sense of humour and a fairly good command of English compared to the others.

In the morning, we showed Ali what we had in our fish refrigerator and his eyes would light up when he saw salmon heads in his drawer. Personally, I preferred the turbot collars, but it was all really tasty. We would observe their cooking technique, which involved a pan with a lot of oil in the middle of the stove, a lot of onions and the spice mix and fish. The rapid cooking seemed to emulsify the natural liquids and spices. This was the closest I got to proper Indian home cooking, obviously with the most carefully chosen ingredients.

These days I tend to cook Indian or Asian food at home when entertaining and usually experiment with dishes from a range of restaurant experiences. I find the different use of spices with different ingredients fascinating. I've even perfected onion bahjis and pakoras, and passed on the technique to Robin Hutson, as at most restaurants they are way too stodgy and don't have a nice crisp texture.

Fish curry

Serves 4–6

My favourite part of the fish to use for this curry is the actual collar, as technically it's a by-product or off-cut and it has a nice gelatinous texture. Fish cheeks also work well in this recipe. If you don't have enough fresh fish of your own, ask your fishmonger to save fish collars for you from fish such as cod, haddock, halibut or turbot – you can freeze them until required. Alternatively, you can ask your fishmonger for any fish heads from large species, then cut out the collars and cheeks and use the rest for stock.

1.5kg (3lb 5oz) fish collars

60g (2¼oz) ghee or vegetable oil

1 teaspoon cumin seeds

½ teaspoon fenugreek seeds

1 teaspoon ground cumin

1 teaspoon grated turmeric root or
   1 teaspoon ground turmeric

Pinch of saffron threads

1 teaspoon curry powder

Good pinch of curry leaves

½ teaspoon ground paprika

1 teaspoon fennel seeds

1 teaspoon mustard seeds

3 medium onions, roughly chopped

5 large garlic cloves, crushed

1 tablespoon chopped fresh root ginger

3 small, medium-strength chillies,
   deseeded and finely chopped

2 teaspoons tomato purée

2 tablespoons lemon juice

1.3 litres (2¼ pints) hot fish stock (1 good-
   quality fish stock cube dissolved in that
   amount of hot water is fine)

3 tablespoons chopped fresh coriander
   leaves

Salt and pepper

Basmati rice, to serve

Season the fish collars to taste with salt and pepper. Heat half the ghee/ vegetable oil in a large, heavy-based pan and fry the fish on a high heat until lightly coloured. Remove the fish with a slotted spoon and put to one side.

Add the rest of the ghee/vegetable oil to the pan and fry all the spices on a low heat until they begin to colour. Add the onions, garlic, ginger and chillies, then cook with the lid on for 4–5 minutes, stirring occasionally, until the onions soften.

Add the tomato purée, lemon juice and stock, bring to the boil, season to taste again and simmer for 45 minutes. Take a cupful of the sauce from the pan, blend in a blender until smooth and pour it back into the sauce. Add the fish and simmer for 15 minutes, then add the coriander and simmer for a further 5 minutes, seasoning once more, if necessary. Serve with basmati rice.

* * *

Over the years, I've been introduced to good fishing spots in London like the Regent's Canal. It used to puzzle me exactly what the anglers were fishing for, except for old shopping trolleys, but I later discovered there are good-sized pike lurking beneath the still, murky water. Andy Kress also introduced me in the early days to Walthamstow Reservoirs, on the outskirts of London, where there is a good amount of brown and rainbow trout along with other coarse species, plus pike in the River Lea alongside the reservoirs.

Andy also used the vast reservoirs to teach and guide me on casting. They were the perfect spot because there aren't too many snags on your back cast. I also caught a few trout while practising the casting, which was an added bonus.

On one particular occasion, I went up to the reservoir on my Vespa with my rod strapped to my back, and on arrival the reservoir attendant said, 'There's no fish, sadly.' I asked what he meant. He replied, 'The Polish have been jumping the fence at night and fishing with long lines and cleared us out.' Blimey, I've never heard of long lining in rivers; netting, yes, by my old school chums, but long lining is a saltwater fishing method that uses hundreds of baited hooks for cod and whatever else takes the bait, not little trout (although they were probably fishing for carp, as it's a common table fish in Eastern Europe). This was urban poaching for food, and it most certainly messed up the fishing for a season or so.

9.

Scotland

Steak tartare on the train

On an annual Dumfriesshire trip some years back to visit my friends Ben and Silvia Weatherall, we had the pleasure of Harold McGee's company, a well-known food scientist who had some influence on Heston Blumenthal's cooking and methodology. I'd never met him, as was the case for many of the others in the party, so each of us took it in turns to pick his brains when the time was right. There was a good, fun crowd, including food writer and journalist Matthew Fort, chef Fergus Henderson and my other fishing buddy, Andy Kress.

For a change, I was the only one to catch a salmon. It was on my first fish on the River Nith and the salmon was destined to be our celebratory supper. The rules on the Nith are that you can keep your first fish; otherwise I would have returned it. But as the salmon was going to a good table of foodies, it made sense to keep it and was indeed appreciated by all.

A year or so before, I'd bought Ben and Silvia a lovely, large, vintage copper fish kettle, which I bought from Mitch Tonks. It was taking up precious space in his small restaurant, The Seahorse, in Dartmouth, Devon. The fish kettle that Ben and Silvia had for years was a bit small and only fit for smaller fish, plus living so close to their own stretch of the river and a plentiful supply of fish, they often had to cut fish in half to poach them.

My kitchen assistant for the supper was Andy. Ben had some grouse to hand and a few different birds that he needed clearing, which we made into a broth with some young root vegetables and greens from Silvia's kitchen garden. As I scaled and gutted the salmon ready for the kettle, I discovered eggs, which I felt a little guilty about, but it's difficult to know with most fish, unless it's a lobster or prawn, when the eggs are easy to detect under the tail. These are most certainly always returned.

So I suddenly thought: why not create fresh salmon caviar with a brine of sea salt and maybe a splash of sherry or something, and serve it on half a baked potato? Well, why not? So I got a handful of Cornish sea salt and carefully mixed it with the eggs and sherry. Then occasionally over the next few hours I broke the eggs down with my hands as the connecting membranes broke down. In the restaurants, we often do baked potato with caviar for special events. We use caviar from Mottra Caviar who produce sustainable caviar in Riga, the capital of Latvia. The fish are milked for their eggs and not killed, so they produce eggs for years to come. The caviar was looking good and the odd taster to check if it needed more salt or more sweetness from the sherry proved satisfying.

Next day, Silvia was cooking a roast sirloin from their herd of Galloway cattle. Harold, Peter Weeden and myself had to head back to London before lunch and didn't want to risk the food on the train, so I asked Silvia if I could take off a piece of beef before it went into the oven. I chopped it finely, and then got together all the ingredients for steak tartare and some of Silvia's good old-fashioned Melba toast. Ben kindly gave us a bottle of claret and we set off for the train with all the kit.

As the ticket guard approached our table with a curious smile, I was tossing the steak tartare together with the other ingredients while Peter was cracking open the claret. I offered him some, but his expression suggested raw beef wasn't quite his thing. This, of course, wasn't exactly a riverbank feast, and I bet we were the only people on a train anywhere mixing a steak tartare for lunch. I do quite often do my own little train buffet when travelling, and have done all sorts of things, from caviar with blinis to a lobster salad with Japanese dressing, but this was a first for the steak tartare. I suppose in my line of business it's easy to knock up luxurious and extravagant food to go, so why not.

Stary Dom steak tartare

Serves 4

Stary Dom is a large traditional Warsaw brasserie with lots of theatre going on at the tables in an old-fashioned way that you rarely see any more. Their preparation of steak tartare at the table is like seeing a skilled Japanese chef at work, slicing and chopping the fillet with razor-sharp accuracy. When I visited earlier in the year, the Stary Dom steak tartare added pickled mushrooms, which was really very good, and I've borrowed that idea several times. Pack your chopped beef on ice in a cool-bag before you head off fishing – or to catch the train.

500g (1lb 2oz) very fresh lean fillet, sirloin or topside steak

2–3 medium shallots, very finely chopped

50g (1¾oz) capers, drained, rinsed and chopped

50g (1¾oz) gherkins, finely chopped

100g (3½oz) white button mushrooms or penny buns (ceps/porcini), trimmed, finely chopped and marinated in 2 tablespoons cider vinegar for 2–3 hours

2 teaspoons Worcestershire sauce

1 tablespoon olive oil

Salt and pepper

To serve:

Leafy salad

Melba toast or ordinary toast

153

With a very sharp chopping knife, slice the beef as finely as possible. Mix all the ingredients together and season to taste with salt and pepper. You may wish to add a little more Worcestershire sauce, or some of the other ingredients – it's up to you. Spoon the steak tartare on to a plate or, if you prefer, push it into a ring mould. Serve with a leafy salad and either Melba toast or ordinary toast.

Caviar baked potatoes

Serves 4

If you are going to incorporate caviar into a recipe, then it needs to be simple and not just used as a garnish where it serves no purpose and just teases the palate. A good old baked potato with excessive amounts of butter mashed into it is perfect. The heavenly and slightly salty flavour of caviar works perfectly spooned on to a humble earthy tuber. I've made these baked potatoes in various forms over the years with caviar and salmon caviar (keta), and also miniaturized them in size to canapés and snacks.

4 small baking potatoes, about 200–250g (7–9oz) each

60–70g (2¼–2½oz) unsalted butter

½ tablespoon chopped chives

60g (2¼oz) Mottra Caviar or salmon caviar (keta)

Salt and pepper

Preheat the oven to 180°C (350°F), Gas Mark 4. Place the potatoes on a tray and bake for about 1 hour, or until soft. Leave the potatoes to cool, then cut them in half. Scoop the potato into a bowl, keeping the skins, and mash with the butter and chives. Season to taste with salt and pepper. Place the skins on a tray, with the scooped-out sides facing down, and rub with a little butter. Return the skins to the oven for about 10 minutes, or until crisp. To serve, refill the skins with the mashed potato and spoon the caviar over the potato until well covered.

Hot-stone salmon on the River Nith with Ben and Silvia

Over the years, I've discovered that fishing trips to Ireland and Scotland need to be a bit spontaneous, as often when I've spent hours on the train or plane there hasn't been enough rain, meaning the river level is too low and the fish aren't running. Or it's been completely the opposite – there's been too much rain, the river has completely flooded, the water is brown and the fishing is also a complete right-off.

A few years ago, on a trip to visit Ben and Silvia Weatherall (*see* page 151), the River Nith flooded. Ben drove Andy Kress and me to a bridge close by. We watched hundreds of small and large salmon in the pool below the waterfall, 50–60m (164–197ft high), trying to work their way up to access the river above for their onward journey. It was fascinating and we spent a couple of hours just observing the successful and unsuccessful efforts of these determined salmon. This certainly made up for not fishing. Neither of us had ever witnessed anything quite like it in our fishing days. The two of us were taking videos on our iPhones and sending them to our fishing buddies. We could have easily got close to the pool, cast a fly and caught one, as there were so many fish, but we resisted.

On one particular trip to the Weatherall's for a spot of salmon and sea trout fishing, Ben reckoned the river was going to be perfect and that the fish would be running. He had given me the nod at short notice and I was fortunately free. It was all a bit speculative, but all I could do was say that the suggestion was great and I'd see him next week. I must say, unlike in Ireland, I've not always blanked completely on my visits to Dumfriesshire, so on each trip to Ben's over the years I have hoped for a fish.

Depending on the time of year there's also the opportunity of a bit of grouse shooting with the dogs on Ben's brother Percy's grouse moor, so if the river fails us, we are almost always sure of a highly prized game bird for supper. We can also forage for some blaeberries and wild mushrooms – a Macnab in a slightly different way, I suppose, having never shot a deer (*see* page 182).

Ben and Silvia are the best hosts. Silvia is a keen gardener, with a walled garden full of everything you need for an off-the-hoof supper, so it's always a joy cooking with whatever we shoot, catch or forage. We always end up with a good supper back at their house, or a sophisticated barbecue on the riverbank next to their recently purchased gypsy caravan.

On the first morning, I caught a nice-sized grilse (a young salmon), and as we'd planned to have supper outside, I had an idea. I dug a shallow hole and placed three large rocks from the riverbank in among some charcoal and bits of wood, as they may well have done centuries ago before barbecues. I gutted the fish, washed it in the river and cut it into three chunks. I found some seasoning in the caravan, and seasoned and lightly oiled the chunks of grilse. I'd never cooked in this way before and was slightly concerned that the stones might explode with the heat, but they didn't. The fish was cooking nicely, with occasional careful turning, and the stones seemed to be pretty nonstick with the heat. The fish didn't loose a single piece of skin and crisped up nicely.

This was a slightly medieval but revolutionary way to cook salmon – or anything for that matter – that we hadn't pre-empted prior to putting our waders on and getting in the river. This is one of the things I love about cooking 'on the hoof': you never quite know what you're going to catch, and in this case, how you are going to cook it. I'm sure this primitive method of cooking existed centuries ago or more, and if I hadn't caught the grilse, it may well have been some of Ben's Galloway beef or Blackface lamb that he rears in the surrounding area.

I cooked some whole young leeks from the garden in among the coals while the salmon was cooking, which the Spanish traditionally do with large spring onions called *calçots*, and we had those with the salmon (*see* page 98 for my recipe for Blackened Leeks with Romesco Sauce).

10.

Ireland

Blanking on the Blackwater with a purple fly in my cheek

As you may have worked out by now, my trips aren't all about catching fish. There's fun and games to be had when the water is too high or too low, or whatever other reasons the gillie, or riverkeeper, gives you when no one is catching anything. Well, that casting practice certainly made me 'match-fit' for an autumn salmon trip on the Blackwater River in County Cork in the Republic of Ireland.

We were a party of five keen fishermen and gastronauts: Robin Hutson, Peter Hannan, Travers Nettleton and Ashley Levett, a commodities trader and entrepreneur. We all fish a lot – well, quite a bit – and travel to where the fish, fun and culture take us.

Whenever I travel with fishing kit and watch the bag go into that oversized hole at the airport, I'm always slightly dubious as to whether it's going to get to its final destination. Although this had never happened before, there's always a first time. When we got to County Cork airport, after flying from Heathrow, we waited and waited and waited – and that was it: no rods and fishing kit, oh no. So that was a first, but hey, we had 16 hours before we fished and a few phone calls ensured the kit was sent on the next flight and dropped at the house where we were staying.

On our arrival at Justin and Jenny Green's Ballyvolane House hotel, which is a fantastic spot to spend a quiet weekend fishing or shooting, our two gillies, Norman and Martin, were in the car park to greet us, wearing semi-serious smiles. They announced that there were no fish in the river, and only one fish had been caught so far that year. Well, that was similar to the situation I'd encountered visiting the same place and fishing there a few years ago with chef Richard Corrigan – and we had blanked then. This time, there was hardly any water in the river – quite the reverse of the scenario on my recent Iceland trip (*see page 180*) – which, in fishing terms, means the fish can't run the river to reach their spawning destination. So they hold up in the saltwater estuary where they are near impossible to catch unless you have a net. Rivers need rain and so this can be a common problem with salmon fishing, but it's hard to judge when you pre-plan a trip. Always best to live on the river, I suppose!

Later in the day, Peter arrived across the border from County Antrim in Northern Ireland armed with a cool-box of his very fine meats, which included 1kg (2lb 4oz) of porterhouse steak, plus big old ribs of aged beef, racks of lamb and *guanciale*. I had brought a couple of sides of our own smoked salmon and, to wash it all down, Peter had loaded a couple of cases of red, pre-empting our traditional lunchtime riverside desires.

Day one, arrival day, we had a spontaneous, short, two-hour fish in the early evening before dinner at Ballyvalone. I borrowed a rod and had a brief but exiting encounter with a salmon that chased my little purple shrimp fly across the surface, then disappeared and was off down the river somewhere. So on the first short fish we all blanked, but the brief chase was encouraging, to say the least, even if it was the only bit of excitement of the week!

Day two, we split up into two groups with our gillies. It was all going well in a non-fishy kind of way and Chris, our photographer, was shooting away for an *Esquire* magazine piece I was writing. He was ready to snap our first fish, along with various casting techniques using single and double-handed rods, when a sudden gust of wind on my line as I lifted off the water, trying to avoid Chris, swung the same purple shrimp fly that was chased by the salmon the day before straight into my right cheek. It was a slow-motion moment as I saw the damn thing coming straight at me, and there was not a thing I could do about it. I turned to Martin, the gillie, and he suggested trying to get it out with the degorging gadget in his fishing waistcoat. Then, on closer inspection, he shook his head and said, 'No, lad, it's well in. Two out of three treble hooks – come with me to the surgery.' This was a bloody first for me, and the reason why you should always wear glasses for fishing: one, to see the fish, and two, not to get the fly in your eye!

Surprisingly, it didn't hurt, but there was some pain to come for sure, as the hooks were lodged in my cheek, according to Martin who had never seen that before, with some of the quickly snipped-off fly line attached. Some people I know would pay good money for a face piercing like that, and with such a colourful and decorative piece (*see* page 1 of this book for evidence).

We just managed to catch Dr Barry before he left the surgery – and no queue! Well, off with me waders and shirt and on to the inspection bed. He too shook his head and said he'd never seen two hooks embedded like that before, which worried me a bit, although there was not a lot I could do about it at that point. After administering a syringe of local anaesthetic in my face, he called for Martin's assistance. He was in the waiting room because he didn't want to come in and watch the operation. The Doc sent Martin across the road to the mechanics to borrow a pair of pliers for the operation, as he said there would be a fair bit of snipping and tugging to be done – eek! I know how a bloody salmon feels now. Whatever he pumped into me certainly numbed my cheek sufficiently while the Doc and Martin were pulling and clipping the hooks one at a time.

By the time I returned from the Doc's, the barbecue was lit and Peter's 100-day-aged beef was sitting on a board ready for me to cook. The boys must have had faith in the Doc and my ability to perform on the barbi semi-conscious. What a sterling job Doc Barry did; there were just two red dots on my cheek after all that, but he did warn me it would be a bit blue and sore the following day. Anyway, I got straight back into my waders and into the river for a quick hour's fish, with a different fly of course, as I'd run out of purple shrimps, while the barbecue warmed up.

Lunch became a bit of a snapping frenzy – and Twitter and Instagram moment – me with five ribs of beef, each weighing 1kg (2lb 4oz) on the barbecue, and a frying pan of last night's sliced-up, leftover potatoes, greens and chopped spring onions, looking like a traditional Irish champ with a big old white patch on my cheek. The two gillies hadn't seen anything like it.

Peter's beef is very special due to his Himalayan salt-ageing process, which allows the beef to mature while not developing mould on the exterior (*see* page 167). So whether it's your standard 28 days, or 100 days in this case, the beef stays the same and you don't get any of that blue-cheese-like exterior, as happens with a lot of aged beef. Eight bottles of Peter's Gigondas later, with 5kg (11lb) of Hannan's Himalayan salt-aged beef inside us, we thought sod the fishing, as it looked as if we were not going to make much contribution to the single fish catch this year – and we didn't want any more casualties.

Next morning, just as I was tucking into smoked salmon and

scrambled eggs at the breakfast table with the boys, the Doc called to check if I was OK. Now, I'm not sure that would happen in the UK. I had the pleasure of telling him there was surprisingly no pain or bruising following the foul-hooking incident, and the big white patch was off. He then confessed that when he got home and told his wife the story, she produced one of my cookbooks from the kitchen shelf – nice.

The fishing didn't get any better. We even tried out the mouth of the estuary for sea bass and ended up with a bucketful of mackerel, which, of course, wasn't the targeted species for the week, but better than blanking completely, I suppose.

On my previous trip with Richard Corrigan, we went to O'Brien's Chop House in Lismore, near Waterford in County Cork in the Republic of Ireland. Just as we approached the front door, Justin was leaning on the frame. He greeted us and said, 'Mark, we haven't met before, but I have a confession before you come in.' Oh dear, I thought, smiling, who's he got in there? A poached member of staff maybe, an ex-girlfriend, who knows? Justin smiled and said to come on in, so we did and went to the bar. He said, 'I love your Oyster & Chop House in Smithfield, everything about it, and I couldn't help but borrow a few ideas from you.' As he spoke, I followed his eyes around the room. I laughed and clocked a few objects such as glug glug jugs, copper and silverware, and pewter tankards. I smiled and said that he really did get some influence from me and that I was flattered, thank you. 'Let's have dinner in the garden,' he said. So off we went to his beautiful walled garden. Single A4 menus in plastic folders were placed in front of us. I said to Justin, 'I nicked the menu idea from Chez l'Amis Louis, in Paris, so we are even-steven.'

100-day-aged porterhouse steak with chimichurri

Serves 2–4

The chimichurri is a great Argentinian salsa to serve with simple grilled meats or fish – or vegetables, come to that.

1 porterhouse steak, weighing about 1kg (2lb 4oz)

Olive oil, for brushing

Sea salt flakes and coarsely ground black pepper

For the chimichurri:

2 handfuls of fresh coriander, finely chopped

Handful of parsley, finely chopped

3 garlic cloves, crushed (wild garlic leaves/ ramson can be used instead when in season)

2 large shallots or 4 small shallots, finely chopped

100ml (3½ fl oz) olive oil

Finely grated zest and juice of 1 lime

Sea salt and pepper

Preheat the barbecue. To make the chimichurri, put all the ingredients in a food processor and process until fairly coarse. Brush the steak with some olive oil and season to taste with sea salt and black pepper. Cook the steak for 3–4 minutes on each side on the hottest part of the barbecue so that it colours nicely, then move to a cooler part and finish cooking the steak until done to your liking – this will obviously depend on the thickness of the steak.

Glenarm Estate

I've got to know Randal McDonnell, Viscount Dunluce, who owns Glenarm Castle in Country Antrim, Northern Ireland, over the years via Peter Hannan, who produces fine-quality beef on the Glenarm Estate. I was lucky to meet Peter when I first opened HIX Oyster & Chop House in 2008. He complimented me on my beef, but said he could do better. We promised to keep in touch and I finally visited him on the Glenarm Estate.

Peter showed me his first experimental Himalayan salt chamber for ageing beef. This is basically a temperature-controlled, walk-in, meat-hanging chamber with a wall of salt bricks. Peter had worked out that the pink rock salt from the Himlayas, which has been underground for a very long time, conditions the air, encouraging good bacteria and killing off bad bacteria. Used in the meat chamber, the rock salt stops the ageing beef going mouldy.

The clever salt bricks and persistent monitoring by Peter's team control the growth of bacteria as the meat matures, meaning that the end-user does not have to trim the meat of mould before cooking. Anyway, the result is matured beef of an exceptional quality. Peter and I then agreed that my restaurants would have UK exclusivity to his beef (although we have OK'd a couple of close friends, namely Mitch Tonks and Angela Hartnett, to use it, too).

What has this beef stuff got to do with fishing, you may be asking yourself? Quite simply, through Peter I met Randal Dunluce who owns the 20-odd farms on and around the Glenarm Estate where the beef is carefully selected. That meant more trips to Ireland. I asked Peter about fishing and discovered that he held the world spey-casting record many years ago, so then the fishing conversations started. We now fish together every year, sometimes with Robin Hutson, sometimes with Andy Kress and André Lima de Luca, our Brazilian master of meat and fire, who flies over especially for the occasion.

In those years we have fished in all sorts of locations in the Republic of Ireland in the hope of nailing a salmon. We choose the locations based on Peter's promises of where he has fished successfully and on local experts' recommendations. Well, over the past seven years or eight, we haven't caught a damn thing, except for when we go out on Judd Rusne's boat and catch small sea trout near the mouth of the River Moy. I'm convinced that one day we will catch an Irish salmon. I'm determined to, and if I have to go twice a year to increase the chances, I will!

Fishing on Judd's boat is a dead cert catching-wise, even if it's only half a dozen fish, as this is the first part of the sea trout run up the River Moy. We anchor up mid-river, so the fish have to swim under the boat. Judd fishes for mackerel out at sea and uses firm, fatty mackerel belly cut into strips and lightly salted for the sea trout bait.

Traditionally, when it comes to lunch, Judd drives the boat up on to the sand on a little island. We light a barbecue and Judd cooks the fish whole in foil with salt and lots of ground white pepper and butter. We grill a few Glenarm lamb chops, drink beer and wine, and talk nonsense! The sea trout fishing with Judd has saved the day every time – cheers Judd.

On returning to the Glenarm Estate to cook a beefy dinner, I always like to have a little fish on Randal's river. Again, I had another Irish salmon blank, but walking back to the house with Randal's young lad Alexander, I spotted a huge puffball mushroom sitting on the lawn under a tree to the left of the house. In case you've never seen a puffball, it's a huge white ball, as the name suggests. On average, puffballs are the size of a football, but they can get much, much bigger. This one was probably about four times the size of a football, no exaggerating. I pointed it out to Alexander and he ran over to pick it up – it was the size of his upper body. That's breakfast sorted, I said to him. He gave me an unsure smile and said, 'Are we going to eat it?' I replied that we would – what else would we do with a prize mushroom like that? I explained that we could barbecue it, then pop a fried duck's egg and some of Peter's crispy sugar pit bacon on top.

Barbecued puffball with fried duck's eggs and bacon

Serves 4

If you can't get your hands on a puffball, then you can replicate this dish using four large field mushrooms. Feel free to use *guanciale* or pancetta instead of the bacon, if you prefer. I have suggested using a barbecue to cook this dish, but you can, of course, simply grill the mushroom and fry the bacon and eggs at home if you wish.

4 slices of puffball or 4 large field
mushrooms, about 2–3cm
(¾ –1¼ inches) thick
3–4 tablespoons rapeseed oil, for brushing
and frying

8–12 streaky bacon rashers
Good knob of butter
4 free-range duck eggs
Salt and pepper

Preheat the barbecue. Brush the slices of puffball/field mushrooms with rapeseed oil and season to taste with salt and pepper. Grill the slices of mushroom for 2–3 minutes on each side until nicely coloured, brushing with more oil if necessary. Meanwhile, cook the bacon rashers until crisp, either directly on the barbecue or in a frying pan. Heat a little oil in the same or a different frying pan, add the butter and gently fry the eggs on a low heat on the barbecue (or on a hob indoors) until just set, then slide on to the mushrooms and serve with the crispy bacon.

Sea urchin supper and breakfast

You don't need to go fishing to enjoy the fruits of the sea, although I very rarely have a trip to the seashore without fishing the local water. When I stayed with my friend Thomas Dane, an art dealer, in Caherdaniel in County Kerry in the Republic of Ireland a few years ago, I couldn't help but notice the sea urchin shells washed up on the shore among the rocks while I was out fishing off the Lamb's Head peninsula.

The fishing was a bit grim and we only caught a couple of small pollack, so I asked the guys from a diving school just near us in the tiny harbour if they would mind grabbing us some sea urchins. They gave us a rather 'you must be mad' look, to say the least, and asked what we were going to do with them. 'Eat them, of course!' we replied promptly. Then they really did think we were crazy Englishmen, as it was obviously not a local delicacy and only for hardened seafood extremists like ourselves.

I got on the phone to a couple of Irish chef friends and Richard Corrigan confirmed that the local sea urchins were just fine to eat. The divers got us a couple of carrier bags full and wouldn't accept any payment, so off we went back up to the house for a seafood feast. Thomas had bought some local lobsters, and I got busy cleaning the sea urchins of their spines and then cutting them in half with a pair of scissors to reveal their delicious orange interiors.

We ate the sea urchins as a starter, just raw with a teaspoon and a squeeze of lemon. The following morning we used what was left. I simply scrambled some local eggs with butter, folded in the orange sea urchin eggs at the last minute and served the scrambled egg back in the sea urchin shells. I like to make the most of the rare pleasures in life, especially when they are free and local.

A couple of years later, I returned to Thomas's house with the family and armed with a bit more local knowledge. Again, I had little success on the fishing front, although as usual I tried every opportunity, including some sea trout fishing on Lough Currane, also in County Kerry.

We ended up going to the tiny harbour at the end of the Lamb's Head peninsula and pleading with a couple of local fishermen to sell us the only two lobsters they had. They had already promised them to someone else, unfortunately, but I did see a large pollock in the net, for which they wouldn't accept any money – they probably thought I was going to use it as bait. In fact, pollock is one of my favourite fish and also very sustainable, so I guess Lamb's Head must be an opportune spot for free seafood.

Scrambled eggs with sea urchins

Serves 4

If you can't fish for fresh sea urchins, you'll probably need to order some in advance from your fishmonger, as they are not as common on the fishmonger's slab in England as they are in some other countries – unless you know a friendly diver, that is. As for the eggs, I like to use Burford Browns because the yolks have a nice rich flavour and are really yellow, which gives the scrambled eggs a beautiful colour.

4 fresh sea urchins

50g (1¾oz) butter

6 eggs, beaten

2 tablespoons double cream

Salt and freshly ground white pepper

To prepare the sea urchins, wear a sturdy pair of gloves and use a kitchen knife to scrape away all the spines from the shells. Give the shells a good wash. Use a pair of scissors to make a hole just above the middle line of each sea urchin, then carefully snip around the shell so that you have 2 halves – one half will be empty and the other will contain orange eggs in segments. With a teaspoon, carefully remove only the orange eggs and put them in a bowl. Discard the rest of the sea urchin inside the shells and give the shells a good wash and scrub. Put the shells in a saucepan, cover with water, bring to the boil and simmer for a couple of minutes to sterilize them. Drain the shells and give them a final wash, removing any membrane, then dry them off.

Melt the butter in a saucepan, add the beaten eggs and season to taste with salt and white pepper. Cook over a low heat, stirring continuously, until the eggs begin to set. Stir in the double cream and cook for another 30 seconds. Stir in the sea urchin eggs, remove from the heat and spoon the scrambled egg into the warmed shells. Serve immediately.

11.

Rest of the World

A cod feast and some scallops in Norway

I'd never been to Norway before, and in 2018 I went on a three-day trip with Val Warner and Ailana Kamelmacher. We stayed in Holmen with Ingunn and Trondheim Rasmussen in their boutique lodge hotel, Holmen Lofoten. We were planning to do a series of chef visits with like-minded friends in the business, who would be hosting a few days' cooking, and also to enjoy some fishing, hunting and bird-watching – my friend Oliver Rampley, the bird-watching expert, would be there.

A lot of Norway is like Holmen and the surrounding villages, where it's all about the cod, as that's the main industry it would seem. There are big wooden racks on the sides of the roads, some with cod heads drying and some with the bodies. The cod is dried for months on end, and then exported to North America, Africa and Southeast Asia. It's the type of stuff you see and smell in African and Caribbean markets, which is then sold and reconstituted for dishes like the classic salt cod fritters and salt cod salads.

We persuaded Trondheim to take us out on his boat to get a cod or two for supper. Val had been before, and I'd heard his stories of filling the boat up with cod, so it was not an opportunity to be missed. Our tackle was heavy-duty, and much heavier than my Dorset sea bass and cod gear, and our pirks (cod lures) weighed about 500g (1lb 2oz) each. These had to be retrieved at speed once you hit the bottom. Back in Dorset, our cod pirks weigh about 150g (5½oz) max, so these boys were pretty taxing on all the muscles you never thought you had.

We headed just a few miles offshore – you don't need to go too far out for cod because the water gets deep pretty close to shore. However, as it wasn't the height of the season, we didn't really bag up on fish, which we would have done a few months later. But we certainly caught enough for supper. Val and I were mentally creating dishes that would use every bit of the cod as we fought them to the surface, which felt a long old way up. We also caught the odd saithe (or coalfish), which is in the same family as the pollack and actually quite difficult to tell apart.

Lots of my friends talk about the cod fishing in Norway and the abundance of fish. We had a modest catch – maybe ten fish between us – although that was a pretty exhausting experience nevertheless. I couldn't wait to get into the kitchen to prepare dinner and relax with a cold beer.

Val and I prepared the cod on the quay by the boat, so the kitchen wouldn't get too messy. We filleted the cod, divided up the top loins, tails and belly, and removed the cheeks, putting them to one side with the chitterlings. These are the unformed male roe and are delicious. The beauty of dissecting fish is that you can see exactly what you have. All the heads and bones went straight into a big saucepan, ready to go off to the kitchen to get a stock on, while we confirmed the dishes and swigged a couple more local beers.

The Norwegians aren't that adventurous with their cod, so Val and I were quite chuffed with our dissection of the catch – we wanted to show the locals a thing or two. On our brief two-night stay, we knocked up a couple of suppers with our modest catch, utilizing every bit of the cod we'd caught. From the tails crispy in a broth with ginger to a cod's-head curry, it was all cooked, including the livers to our hosts' surprise – this is where the fun of cooking your own catch comes in.

Our hosts had played safe, in case we didn't catch anything, and bought a box of scallops. I couldn't resist doing something interesting with these for our last breakfast before departure. It was one of those spontaneous moments: the wood- fired oven always seemed to be on the go and we'd had delicious, locally cured bacon the day before, so I thought why not do a little brunch scallop experiment.

I remember my dad cooking scallops and bacon for breakfast once when I was a kid, and this idea had stuck in my head. If you haven't got a wood-fired oven, a conventional oven will do the trick, too. I've found that the scallops cook just nicely in the same time as the eggs (also used in the brunch) without either being overcooked.

Brunch scallops

Serves 4

If only I knew then what I know now, when I would innocently eat anything my dad or grandparents put in front of me. There is something special about eating cured pork and shellfish together – it seems to be the perfect food marriage at any time of day.

½ tablespoon olive or rapeseed oil

4–6 thick streaky bacon rashers, cut into 5-mm (¼-inch) dice, or about 80–100g (3–3½oz) diced pancetta

4 very fresh large scallops, shelled, cleaned and the cupped half-shells reserved

4 eggs

Salt and pepper

Preheat the oven to 200°C (400°F), Gas Mark 6, or use a wood-fired oven, which will be much hotter. Heat the oil in a small saucepan or frying pan and gently cook the bacon/pancetta on a low heat for 2–3 minutes before removing. Meanwhile, detach the roes from the scallops and cut each scallop into 3–4 pieces. Add the scallop pieces and roes to the bacon, and cook on a low heat for a couple of minutes. Divide the scallop pieces between the half-shells, putting them to one side slightly, and season to taste with salt and pepper. Crack an egg beside the scallop in each shell, place the shells on a tray and bake in the oven for about 10 minutes, or until the whites of the eggs are just set. To serve, scatter the bacon and roes over the scallops.

An Icelandic adventure

Salmon were once abundant in many European rivers, but stocks have declined rapidly in places or been completely wiped out. There are several reasons for this. Firstly, there is too much netting and drift-netting going on out at sea. Secondly, the iconic salmon has simply been overfished. This means the popular sport, which is virtually catch-and-release everywhere, is being threatened. Managing these rivers is crucial, and the salmon that make it from the sea to the rivers need to be protected from farm pollution and from poaching (although this is pretty much a thing of the past now). The rivers also need ongoing maintenance, with areas that have been blocked by landfall over the years, for example, being cleared, so that the salmon can reach their spawning sites.

I fish in Iceland most years. I've never caught big numbers of salmon there, but the spontaneous 36-hour trips with Robin Hutson and his business partner Jim Ratcliffe have, ironically, yielded more fish in a day than longer four-day trips with the boys. Over the years, Jim has bought riverside farmland in Iceland – not to farm or build on, but to encourage the farmers to keep farming, with zero rent, and more importantly to preserve the North Atlantic salmon stocks in the rivers.

On the longer trips to Iceland, we take a day off from salmon fishing and go down near the mouth of the River Selá with lighter trout fly rods to fish for Arctic char. This is a fun species to catch, and is closely related to salmon and lake trout. It has the characteristics of both on close inspection, once you get one on the riverbank, that is.

Most salmon-fishing guides have nicknames. Our Arctic char expert was called Sooty, and he supplied us with his own specially tied flies fit for purpose. There's a small window of opportunity to fish when the char run in number up river with the low tide. You literally see them swimming around your waders and are spoiled for choice where to cast. This, of course, doesn't mean they are any easier to catch. I discovered you're better off ignoring the small fish that are teasing you and putting a good cast out into the channel in the hope of catching a larger fish. Although there isn't a catch-and-release policy for char, as there is for salmon, we returned most of our catch and saved some of the larger fish for supper back at the fishing lodge.

My second year fishing with the boys, I bought a fishing trophy on eBay with a pair of leaping bronze salmon and called it the Macnob Trophy. This is like the Scottish fishing/hunting Macnab Challenge, which involves bagging a salmon, a brace of grouse and a deer in the same day. Our trophy was a little less challenging, involving catching a salmon, a trout and an Arctic char in the same day. The challenge certainly added to the suppertime banter among the lads.

Baked Arctic char with honey, mustard and dill

Serves 4–6

I found this recipe in a Russian cookbook. It is rather like a hot baked gravadlax, but without the curing process. You could also use salmon or large sea trout. It makes a great buffet or sharing dish in the centre of the dinner table. The choice of mustard is up to you, although I quite like using Tewkesbury mustard because it has that mild hint of horseradish and the mustard flavour isn't too overpowering. A wood-fired oven is perfect for cooking this dish. In fact, it was originally cooked on short planks of wood that had been soaked in water to prevent them burning and imparting the flavour to the fish. But, obviously, it's fine to just cook the fish in the oven, too.

1 or 2 sides of Arctic char, about 500g (1lb 2oz) each, trimmed, skin left on and boned

2 tablespoons Dijon or Tewkesbury mustard

4–5 tablespoons chopped dill or fennel tops

3–4 tablespoons clear honey

Sea salt and pepper

Preheat the oven to 240°C (475°F), Gas Mark 9. Lay the sides of char on a baking tray, skin side down. Season the fish to taste with sea salt and pepper, spread with the mustard and scatter evenly with the dill/fennel tops. Spoon over the honey and bake in the oven for about 10–15 minutes, keeping the fish just slightly pink. Serve the baked fish hot or at room temperature.

Fishing and hunting in Tuscany

A couple of years back I visited my relatively new friend Oliver Rampley in Florence, Tuscany. Our paths must have been destined to cross, as I was introduced to him at a wedding in Morocco by my friend Lauren, who said, 'How's the fishing? You must meet my friend Ollie. I think you have a lot in common and would get on like a house on fire.' Lauren hooked us up there and then on her phone and, of course, we did meet for dinner and drinks and, yes, we had an awful lot in common.

Ollie seemed to love all the same pastimes as me, except I've never really done any bird-watching, apart from observing seagulls nicking people's lunches down on the Dorset coast. (I bet you thought I was going to be a bit naughty then.) We spent hours eating and drinking, talking fishing and hunting, and I've since introduced him to more like-minded and mad people. We even arrange like-minded people's lunches now, which are usually a mixture of fun and fishing chit-chat – and also potential new Altana business for Ollie (*see* page 21).

On our first proper date, as it were, Ollie invited me to Florence to see exactly what he gets up to. The prospect of hanging out in a beautiful city and exploring new parts of Tuscany was a fun one indeed. The trip might potentially be one of my most exiting fishing and hunting trips abroad, hopefully to shoot my first wild boar and catch a memorable fish (whatever that might be) – or not, as is often the case.

Having the opportunity to shoot and fish is always exciting, and I often do just that when I visit Ben and Silvia up in Dumfriesshire (*see* page 151), although I haven't yet managed the much-discussed and documented Macnab Challenge of bagging a salmon, a stag and a brace of grouse in one day between dawn and dusk. I've never hunted for deer, but I reckon the opportunity will present itself one day; it's simply a matter of time.

I had a few hours to spare before my flight from London City Airport to Florence, so I strolled down to Columbia Road. It had been a while, as most of my weekends are spent on the Dorset coast. You never quite know what you'll find on the Sunday Columbia Road Flower Market, flowers and plants excluded. Columbia Road is full of interesting shops that come and go, and it lures collectors and hoarders like me. While wandering about, I found a new antiques shop that I hadn't been in before. Would you believe the first thing I spotted, out of the corner of my eye, as I stepped inside were two wild boar glug glug jugs staring at me from a shelf. I'd never seen a boar glug glug jug before, even though I have all sorts of different old designs and colourful fish glug glugs.

I've collected these jugs over the years because of a now-fond childhood memory of the green one my grandmother used to have on her sideboard. I was never very keen on the jug at the time, but in later years I've found them fascinating. They are also extremely useful at dinner parties and as bedside water jugs. It's a bit of a conversation piece, as a lot of people don't know much about them, or where they were made, and that they actually glug as you pour. My little daughter and her friends love pouring water from them, their giggling pre-empting the glugging sound. I've even got different-coloured chicken glug glugs that I've collected since I opened a chicken restaurant called the Tramshed. I also found some tiny Japanese sake ones, which don't glug exactly, but sit nicely on my kitchen shelf among the real glug glugs. Well, maybe this boar jug was some kind of lucky charm, as I was en route to hunt a boar, hopefully successfully. So I bought the pair, being unique little beauties and a perfect welcoming and thank-you gift for Ollie – although I certainly wasn't going to part with both of them, as one was obviously destined for my collection.

A trip to Florence isn't complete without a visit to the famous San Lorenzo Market, which has virtually everything for keen foodies and novice cooks. Italian markets put British ones to shame a bit; the closest we have to this type of market is Borough Market in London's Southwark. Markets are always inspiring, and I always look forward to visiting them in foreign cities, as you just don't know what you're going to find.

The visit to San Lorenzo Market was crucial to our trip, as we had a bit of cooking lined up for the next few days after or during fishing and, with any luck, nailing a wild boar. I had a little shopping wish list on my iPhone notes, but when you're on foreign soil, you never quite know how much of the list will get ticked off. We shopped with intent for my list of essentials, which could potentially be incorporated with whatever we caught. For that potential wild boar, we cheated slightly and pre-ordered a hunter to shoot one, just in case neither Ollie nor I were successful. That's not to say I didn't have full confidence in Ollie after chatting early on in our relationship, but I'm not a confident hunter myself, having only ever shot game birds.

I'd thought getting the essential spices for my curry in the market was going to be tricky, but Ollie said that he knew a trader who would sell us all the spices we needed and we would be fine. I'd heard that before, and Ollie's Italian is pretty damn fluent, but between the two of us and the stallholder it was like the four candles sketch from *The Two Ronnies*.

However, after persevering with the stallholder, we did manage to get ten of the 12 spices on my list, as I wouldn't – and never will – settle for generic curry powder. Ollie now knows the names of crucial curry spices for his kitchen cupboard.

A trip to San Lorenzo Market isn't complete without a visit to the tripe sandwich stand! Da Nerbone sells *trippa* (tripe) or *lampredotto*, which you can eat as a sandwich or in a bun, or on their own. Personally, I prefer to eat them on their own, especially for breakfast. *Trippa* is the edible lining of a cow's stomach, while *lampredotto* is a local Florence speciality. It's the fourth and final stomach of the cow slow-cooked with onions, tomato and celery. The buns are dipped in the sauce and served with a dollop of green sauce and sliced tomatoes. Tripe is classed as peasant food around the world – you either love it or hate it. Most of the people who hate it haven't even tried it, but I'm a big fan and consider it to be more of a luxury dish and a rare treat whenever I can get my hands on the good stuff.

After the inspiring trip around the market and the breakfast tripe treat, I was quite surprised by the amount of fresh Asian ingredients on offer, as there was little evidence of any Asian communities in Florence. I could well have been wrong, though, as the produce at the market did suggest the opposite.

I had another small non-food item on my shopping list. Well, it was a food item in the form of a *fiasco*. A *fiasco* is specific to Tuscany and looks like a wine decanter. A photographer called Jason Lowe, who I used to work with years and years ago, gave me a *fiasco*, but it had broken. It is used for cooking Tuscan beans, specifically beans called *ceccheri*, which look like flattened chickpeas. My poor old flask had broken, but

Ollie reckoned he knew somewhere that would have one close by. He took me to this small hardware store in one of the back streets near the market. Just inside the doors were sacks of different dried beans and pulses, including *ceccheri*. I had to buy a kilo, as they are pretty hard to come by. Ollie asked about the *fiasco* and the lady pointed to a shelf. There was a choice of two, so I bought the same one Jason had bought me, plus a spare top, as they are a bit fragile. Then again, the Tuscans put them in a wood-fired oven overnight when the heat has died down to cook the beans slowly. I was a happy boy, as I hadn't been able to find a *fiasco* or the beans online or anywhere else for love nor money. I like to collect international culinary food gadgets.

After the market and *fiasco* shop, we collected our hire car from just around the corner. We packed everything into a big old cool-box in the boot and headed off to our next destination, Porto Ercole, which is about an hour's drive through the beautiful Tuscan countryside.

Ollie had arranged for me to stay at Hotel Il Pellicano, up in the hills above Porto Ercole, where we were going to be fishing the following day. He knows the owner, Marie-Louise Sciò, the creative mastermind and Italian style icon behind the hotel. It is a classic and sophisticated resort hotel with an awful lot of history and aristocratic background. Back in the 1960s, it would have been a star-studded permanent party place for figureheads from the worlds of music, movies and sport. Sadly, I never met Marie-Louise during my stay, but I felt she was very much in the hotel and present in the simple and stylish design. I'd already had a little insight into Il Pellicano, as I'd bought the book about the hotel photographed by Juergen Teller a few years ago, but had never got round to visiting.

We had dinner in the restaurant on the first night, cooked by chef Sebastiano Lombardi. To my surprise, we were presented with a water list that was two pages long. This was a real first for me and reminded me of the book about water I'd bought from a charity shop in Knightsbridge when I first moved to London. This had a page on each type of water, explaining its source and properties, and gave me an insight into water, being a Dorset lad and not brought up on bottled water – we just drank it straight from the tap. I ended up ordering Speyside, in case you're wondering, followed by a local water called Lauretana.

The menu in the restaurant was an interesting list of Italian classics with a gentle modern touch, without being too fancy. I just couldn't resist the tortellini with rabbit for the second night running, followed by fillet of turbot with chanterelles and a very good spaghetti with lobster and sea urchin, which was luxuriously rich without overloading on the flavours.

Our fishing started early-ish – well, at first light, which is early for most – and before the breakfast brigade in the hotel were on duty, so it was just a swift boat coffee for us. We spent the first hour fishing in the harbour for barracuda and bluefish among the fancy motorboats and yachts. We used light spinning rods and Rapala® lures. I'd never seen or caught a bluefish, only the species in New Zealand, which I assume must have been pretty similar and tasted damn good straight out of the water of the Milford Sound fjord (*see* page 241). To my surprise, ferocious, saltwater, pike-like barracuda are abundant off the coast of this part of Italy. There are certainly plenty of small fish in the harbour for these prehistoric-looking sea scavengers to feed on, along with free food from the local fishing boats in the form of guts and stuff they throw overboard as they prepare fish for the local market.

I'd caught plenty of barracuda in my time in the Bahamas and the Caribbean, but hadn't expected them to be abundant on the Tuscan coast. Within half an hour I'd hooked into a good-sized barracuda. After a good old fight, I got him onboard and on ice in the fish locker. Barracuda fight an awful lot to begin with, and then pretty much give up. In some countries, eating barracuda is forbidden, as they feed on poisonous fish and the coral on reefs, which contain toxins that can be harmful. I experienced this in Barbados and was told not to eat the inshore fish, although in the Bahamas, some of the fishing guides seemed to be keen to take them home. I later learned that the attraction might well be the barracuda's hallucinogenic qualities! Who knows? I wasn't prepared to try this, although did enjoy catching fish in the deep water. Actually, I've eaten a lot of fish over the years and never suffered any side effects.

So that was lunch sorted. To be honest, we had enough for a few lunches and a potential supper because the barracuda weighed 3–4kg (6lb 8oz–9lb) and once filleted provided a good amount of meaty flesh. We then headed out of the harbour and fished for baby garfish to use as live bait, with a method that was completely new to me. This simply involved slowly trolling little lengths of coloured wool with no hooks behind the boat. When the fish attack the lengths of wool, their tiny sharp teeth get stuck and they are then yours to fish with for bigger species.

We had no luck at all out of the harbour and so headed back in, hopefully for some more barracuda sport or possibly a bluefish. I had an epic take on a bluefish, which took off across the harbour at great speed and headed under some mooring ropes. After 15 minutes or so, trying to get the bluefish to swim into clearer water, it sadly snapped the fishing line around a boat's anchor line and was never seen again, but the fight was a lot of fun while it lasted. I must say, we had plenty of action in the harbour and landed a couple of beautiful-looking but smaller bluefish. They were no great size, but certainly good enough for the table and a course in the bag before our next adventure hunting for wild boar.

So, back on the road and off to Alpe della Luna (Alps of the Moon), on the Umbrian-Tuscan border, where Ollie's friends Aurelia and Serenela have a hunting estate. With a boar curry in mind for lunch, we had packed the other ingredients we'd need, including some ginger, chilli and fresh coriander, in a cool-box and popped this in the boot of the hire car. I do love cooking and experimenting with Indian food, and the thought of breaking down a boar carcass was exciting. Also, the fact that the Italians don't eat much curry was a further incentive to knock up an Indian boar feast, so Ollie and I had a good old natter and brainstorm en route. I mean, have you ever seen a curry house in Italy? They are very rare, for sure. Often, if I do find a curry house in Europe, they aren't that good, so we are pretty lucky in the UK where curry is still the most popular meal. Our Italian hunters and guests were hopefully in for a bit of a treat.

Barracuda and pineapple ceviche

Serves 4

I always like to anticipate what I'll cook with a catch, even if the chances of success are slim. In this case, I had a ceviche in mind with whatever we caught, large or small. The barracuda was certainly fairly substantial, and way too much for lunch for the four of us. But we did have another part of the trip where food would be needed if we didn't manage to nail a boar. The shopping in the port had been limited, but I'd spotted a solitary pineapple and some spring onions in a greengrocer's. We'd already bought some fresh coriander and chilli from the market in Florence for the anticipated boar curry feast, so this ceviche was our lunch on the boat, washed down with some tequila that we ordered from the bar at Il Pellicano (*see* page 188).

About 400g (14oz) very fresh white fish fillet, boned and cut into roughly 1-cm (½-inch) cubes

2–3 spring onions, finely chopped

2 green or red chillies, finely chopped

About 200g (7oz) peeled pineapple flesh, cut into roughly 1-cm (½-inch) cubes and any juice reserved

2 tablespoons chopped fresh coriander

Juice of 2–3 limes

1 tablespoon sparkling mineral water

1 tablespoon extra virgin olive oil

Sea salt and pepper

It's important that the ingredients for this ceviche aren't mixed too far in advance, otherwise the fish will cook, so simply mix everything together and season to taste with sea salt and pepper a couple of minutes before you are ready to serve.

Negronis

I first got into negronis about 10 or 12 years ago. I wasn't quite sure of the potent medicinal flavour to begin with, but it eventually grew on me. The negroni has now become my go-to cocktail, as it has for many others, including a fair few girls, which is pretty hardcore, I'd say. I like to serve a big ice sphere or block in my negronis, as it doesn't dilute the drink too much – it's rather like a quick stir on ice for a martini. To be honest, it doesn't really matter what gin you use and there are lots to choose from. Here I give two recipes: one for a standard negroni and one that uses only English ingredients.

Standard negroni

Makes 1

50ml (2fl oz) gin

50ml (2fl oz) Antica Formula Vermouth
  or other red vermouth

50ml (2fl oz) Campari

Ice cubes and an ice sphere

Orange twist or slice, to garnish

Pour all the ingredients into a mixing glass and top up with ice cubes. Stir for 15 seconds, then strain into a tumbler over an ice sphere. Serve with the orange twist or slice.

The Sacred full English negroni

Makes 1

Something I've been aiming at for some time is to create a full English negroni. Thanks to Ian Hart of Sacred Gin, who has also developed a spiced vermouth and rosehip cup, my mission has been accomplished.

30ml (1fl oz) Sacred Gin

20ml (¾fl oz) Sacred English Spiced
  Vermouth

20ml (¾fl oz) Sacred Rosehip Cup

Ice cubes and an ice sphere

1 apple slice, to garnish

Pour all the ingredients into a mixing glass, add some ice cubes and stir for 15–20 seconds, or until the cocktail reaches your desired dilution. Strain into a rocks glass, add an ice sphere and garnish with the slice of apple.

The Fish Terrace at Kalkan in Turkey

I was introduced to Uluc and Claire Bilgutay by Robin Hutson after Robin and his wife Judy had just returned from their 20th annual holiday to Kalkan. Robin always bangs on about what great times they have there, and about the little restaurants, cheap, high-quality fake handbags and, of course, Uluc and Claire's great hospitality. They have a restaurant called The Fish Terrace above the Korsan Meze on the seafront, so I decided to take a mini holiday to Turkey before setting off for Corfu to pick up my daughter. I was taking her back to London for the start of the new school term.

Uluc asked if I would have a look at the menu and kitchen while I was in Kalkan, so of course I did. I'm always fascinated to see what goes on in a Turkish kitchen and had only been to Turkey once very briefly when I visited Istanbul. I took a couple of mornings out and cooked with Uluc, taking a look at some of the current menu dishes. I suggested a few new ones, using local seasonal ingredients that they already had in the kitchen.

It's interesting that countries like Turkey don't often veer away from their traditional cuisine, but I played around with a few dishes, such as serving the squid grilled instead of deep-fried, which every restaurant seems to do. I cooked the squid with bacon and rocket, and served it with a chilli salsa, a dish I used to cook at Le Caprice 25 or so years ago. One of the locally caught fish is amberjack, which has a delicious, meaty flesh, so I dissected the fillet and cooked the thicker top loin blackened, Cajun-style, and the fattier but still very tasty belly with a barbecue marinade baked in corn husks and served with a spiced corn salsa.

There seemed to be a lot of both natural and unnecessary waste in the kitchen, which is always an opportunity to create something extremely cost-effective. So the squid trimmings went into a squid version of Chinese sesame prawn toasts, while the huge amount of watermelon skin, which usually went with all the other vegetable trimmings to Uluc's chickens roaming in his olive groves up in the hills, were turned into preserved watermelon. This was something I'd come across 20-odd years before in South Africa where they serve the watermelon with cheese (*see* page 200 for the recipe). Uluc was delighted that I could turn his chicken food into something edible to complement the soft local cheeses or as a snack.

We were in the height of the watermelon season. You may have noticed that Turkish supermarkets in London have big wooden boxes of watermelons outside. Well, I couldn't resist doing this refreshing watermelon soup, which I'd cooked in the past but not for ages, with the addition of some crispy halloumi. I also used the watermelon in an Asian-inspired crispy sea bream with watermelon salad, as the sea bass and bream are farmed in Turkey and plentiful.

Overall, fresh fish is pretty limited in Turkey. They catch horse mackerel, or scad, which they just call mackerel, that has a great-tasting flesh. We don't really eat this in the UK, but it works a treat as live bait for sea bass and also keeps really well in the live-bait well on a fishing boat. To my surprise, Uluc told me that they catch mahi-mahi off Kalkan, which means that Robin and I may well be taking our vacation at the same time next year.

One lunchtime, after a kitchen session, Uluc and Claire took me on their boat to the restaurant with no name, although everyone calls it

The Fish Shack. It's a 15-minute boat ride, then you anchor up and swim to the shore for lunch, which reminded me of the place we go to religiously in Aix-en-Provence in the South of France for Tracey Emin's birthday. Called Chez Jo, it's on a nudist beach. They have no menu, and serve a huge grouper (or bourgeois, as they call it there) on a big cork platter as a main course. The fish is cooked in a wood-fired oven on a bed of sliced potatoes cooked in fish soup. The Fish Shack serves much smaller fish as main courses and meze starters. Wine is served in an ice bucket made from a large water bottle with the top cut off.

These kinds of places are always at the top of my dining experience list around the world, as you just can't get any better than the hillside view from this little wooden fish shack overlooking the ocean with great company. During our long lunch, we had a few bottles of Turkish wine, which is actually fantastic, especially the Kavaklidere Lal rosé and the Kalecik Karasi red that Uluc drinks chilled – which, as we experienced with the Central Otago Pinot Noirs in Australia (*see* page 243), works perfectly in hot countries.

We swam back to the boat but, sadly, couldn't get the anchor out of the rocks, so had to leave it tied to a buoy to be rescued another day. We fished for a couple of hours up and down the channel, following the local boats, but not, unfortunately, very successfully. We caught a small horse mackerel and an amberjack, so barely enough for supper. I managed to break the tip off my rare, old, eight-piece Hardy smuggler, so that put a stop to our rod-and-line fishing. We had to revert to Uluc's hand line. This is the method used by all the locals, but it isn't as much fun as a bending rod and line when you catch something – which we sadly didn't.

We'd had a similar inland experience the lunchtime before when we were collected by Musa, the restaurant owner, in his car. He took us up into the hills to this Vietnamese-looking shack called the Trout Farm, which actually was a trout farm, surrounded by little flowing streams. There they farm trout naturally and, of course, the no-menu main course was simply cooked trout that Musa brought to the table in the frying pan in which it was cooked. So was the homemade soft cheese starter, which was just sizzling in olive oil with a little chilli. It was actually the best Turkish soft cheese I've ever tasted. It was accompanied by delicious, crispy fried aubergines with a couple of spoonfuls of stewed tomatoes and peppers. Such dishes are often a bit soggy where they've been sitting in the sauce for too long, but these were perfect because they were fried to order and the sauce only spooned over on serving.

Using boats as water taxis is my idea of heaven, and on my last day, Robin treated me to a surprise lunch at Villa Mahal just across the bay. The restaurant is owned by a lovely lady called Ipek who Robin has known for as long he's known Uluc and Claire.

Iced watermelon soup with crispy halloumi

Serves 4–6

Watermelon isn't often used, apart from chopped up and eaten for breakfast or as part of a buffet. I love this soup dish, and it certainly lifts and gives the humble watermelon a different identity. Any type of melon makes a refreshing chilled soup in the summer. You can make the soup with a mixture of varieties, or go for one variety and add a selection of coloured melons at the end.

1kg (2lb 4oz) ripe watermelon (preferably seedless), skinned

A little olive or vegetable oil, for frying

60–80g (2¼–3oz) halloumi cheese, cut into roughly 1-cm (½-inch) pieces

A few mint leaves, to garnish

Cut one-third of the melon into 2-cm (¾-inch) cubes and put in the refrigerator. To make the soup, blend the remaining watermelon in a blender until smooth, then strain through a sieve. Put the soup in the freezer for a couple of hours to give it a slushy consistency, or leave it in the refrigerator overnight. Heat a frying pan just rubbed with some oil and fry the halloumi on a high heat for 1 minute, turning the pieces so that they are evenly coloured, then transfer to a plate lined with kitchen paper. To serve, stir the soup well and spoon into chilled serving bowls. Add the reserved cubes of watermelon and a few pieces of halloumi to each bowl, and garnish with the mint leaves.

Preserved watermelon

Makes enough to fill 2 x 1-litre (1¾-pint) preserving jars

I first came across preserved watermelon at Ken Forrester's 96 Winery Road Restaurant in Stellenbosch outside Cape Town, South Africa. Served with cheese, it was a completely new experience for me. *Waatlemoen konfyt*, as it's known over there, is as traditional to South Africans as Branston pickle is to us. If you've made the Iced Watermelon Soup with Crispy Halloumi (*see* page 199), this is a great way to use up the leftover watermelon skin. As watermelons are big old things, you will get enough skin from just one to fill a good 1-litre (1¾-pint) jar, or even two. I've served preserved watermelon on sticks with cheese, like the classic cheese and pineapple, or you can just put a bowl of it on the table as an alternative to chocolate truffles.

Watermelon skin, leaving about 5mm (¼ inch) of the red flesh

1kg (2lb 4oz) granulated or preserving sugar per 1kg (2lb 4oz) watermelon skin

4 tablespoons lemon juice

40g (1½oz) piece of fresh root ginger, scraped and thinly sliced

2 whole red chillies

First sterilize the preserving jars by removing the rubber rings and putting them through a dishwasher, or by boiling them in a large saucepan of water for 10 minutes or so. Cut the watermelon skin into roughly 2-cm (¾-inch) pieces, put in a saucepan and cover with water. Bring to the boil and simmer for 2 minutes, then drain and repeat the process twice more with fresh water. Put the pieces of watermelon in the pan with the sugar, lemon juice, ginger and chillies. Bring to the boil, then turn down the heat and cook on a medium heat for

45 minutes–1 hour, or until the melon is tender and the liquid is thick and just coating the melon. The water may need topping up during cooking and the temperature adjusting – test the melon with a skewer or the point of a knife. Once cooked, pack the melon into the sterilized preserving jars, cover with the liquid and seal immediately. Allow to cool, then store in a cool, dry place or in the refrigerator.

Catalan broad beans with chorizo

Serves 4

Where Turkey is famous for its delicious meze dishes, in Spain they enjoy similar small dishes called tapas. I've had a dish like these broad beans many times in Spain, and it's often made with trimmings of chopped Iberian ham. The chorizo gives the dish a bit of a kick and makes it a perfect riverbank starter or an accompaniment to a barbecued pork fillet or chop.

2 small onions, finely chopped

4 garlic cloves, crushed

4 tablespoons extra virgin olive oil

90g (3¼oz) small cooking chorizo, halved lengthways and chopped

1 teaspoon tomato purée

500ml (18 fl oz) hot chicken stock (1 good-quality chicken stock cube dissolved in that amount of hot water is fine)

400g (14oz) podded broad beans or good-quality frozen broad beans

1 tablespoon chopped fresh coriander

Salt and pepper

Gently cook the onions and garlic in the olive oil in a saucepan until soft. Add the chorizo, tomato purée and chicken stock. Bring to the boil, season to taste with salt and pepper, and simmer for 45 minutes.

Meanwhile, cook the podded broad beans for 5 minutes in salted boiling water. Allow an extra 2–3 minutes if you're using frozen broad beans. Drain the beans, add to the onion and chorizo mixture and simmer for a further 15 minutes. If the liquid evaporates, add more chicken stock or water. Re-season with salt and pepper, if necessary, then add the coriander and serve.

Souvlaki

Makes 4–6 kebabs

Souvlaki is a popular Greek dish consisting of small pieces of meat on skewers. As well as shoulder of lamb, you can also use pork shoulder or leg, or even under-fillets of lamb. Serve the souvlaki rolled in Greek flatbreads – or, if you prefer, use soft tortillas instead – with sliced tomato and pickled dill cucumbers. If you fancy knocking up some tzatziki, it goes perfectly with these kebabs. Simply peel, deseed and dice half a cucumber, then mix with crushed garlic cloves, a few tablespoons of Greek yogurt, some chopped mint and a splash of olive oil. This is a treat with meat – or as a dip at any time.

1kg (2lb 4 oz) boned shoulder of lamb, trimmed of fat and sinew, then cut into roughly 2-cm (¾-inch) pieces	Salt and pepper
2 tablespoons chopped thyme leaves	**To serve:**
4 garlic cloves, crushed	Flatbreads or soft tortillas
Finely grated zest and juice of 2 lemons	Sliced tomato
300ml (½ pint) olive oil	Picked dill cucumbers
100ml (3½fl oz) red wine	Tzatziki, either shop-bought or homemade (*see* above)

Put the meat in a non-reactive bowl with the thyme, garlic, lemon zest, 100ml (3½ fl oz) of the olive oil and the red wine. Mix well and season to taste with salt and pepper. Cover with clingfilm and leave overnight in the refrigerator. Half an hour before you want to serve, drain the meat and reserve the juices. Whisk the juices with the lemon juice and remaining olive oil in a jar or bowl. Thread the pieces of lamb on to metal kebab skewers and brush with some of the lemon and oil marinade.

Preheat a barbecue or grill, and cook the lamb until slightly pink or medium, if you prefer. This should take no more than 4–5 minutes. Once the lamb is cooked to your required colour, put the pieces of meat in a bowl and leave to rest for about 10 minutes. To serve, brush the flatbreads/tortillas with some of the cooked meat juices from the bowl. Put the flatbreads/tortillas on the barbecue, or under the grill, for 30 seconds or so, but don't let them go crispy. Arrange the lamb on the flatbreads/tortillas with some sliced tomato and picked dill cucumbers, and serve with the tzatziki.

New Orleans
and a trip up the Mississippi River

I've twice been invited to New Orleans by the lovely Carolyn Cavelle, who does the PR for Tabasco sauce, and stayed in her family house on Avery Island where the sauce is made. Tabasco is one of those condiments we take for granted, like tomato ketchup and Worcestershire sauce, and most households and every bar and pub have it. The tour around the Tabasco factory is fascinating and a must if you find yourself in that part of the world.

I always learn a thing or two in places such as these and come away with a few inspired ideas. Tom Parker Bowles and I managed to persuade our hosts to give us some of the pepper mulch that's left after the fermentation and pressing, so we walked away with two vacuum-packed parcels to take home and experiment with. It looks a bit like a coarse harissa, but has a delicious, fiery taste, as you can imagine. While in New Orleans being entertained by the Tabasco family, we ate some fantastic Creole dishes such as jambalaya, gumbo and po'boys (baguettes filled with fried meat or seafood), for which the area has a great reputation, and, of course, proper whiskey sours.

One of the most memorable days was a trip up the Mississippi River on a boat wearing our Tabasco hats, flip-flops and T-shirts – and whatever else had tempted us in the factory shop. We thought we were just going for a trip up the river, then the boat slowed down and turned into some reeds. A blues and jazz band were playing for us in front of a wooden lodge where two big pots of water were boiling away. This was a surprise lunch for us. A couple of guys were sat on stools by the boilers, cooking bucket after bucket of crayfish. We sat at long wooden tables, and the buckets of crayfish were literally tipped down the middle and then placed on the floor for collecting the shells. This was some feast. We couldn't eat the crayfish quick enough before the next bucket was tipped on to the tables. The staff put plastic bibs around the customers when they sit down, as this type of crayfish feasting is quite messy. This was a unique and delicious experience in a perfect setting.

We washed the crays down with beer and whiskey sours, which were flowing by the pitcher load. If we'd been in Scandinavia, we would have been washing them down with shots of aquavit. While shopping in New Orleans one day and munching on an oyster po'boy, I couldn't resist buying a box of crab and crawfish boil sachets, not so much for what was inside, but for the box itself: it was a beautiful, classically branded and yellow. I've never used the contents and the box is, in fact, now an ornament in my kitchen library, next to my Italian chitarra machine, a musical-looking wooden string instrument that's used for cutting pasta. I love collecting stuff like that.

We asked our amazing hosts if there was any good fishing close by, and the following afternoon we were taken to a lake with freshwater bass and largemouth bass, neither of which I'd caught before. It's a bit confusing, as the saltwater striped bass and the UK's native sea bass don't really resemble these freshwater species, but there is also a freshwater striped bass. All the freshwater species grow to a fair size and are ferocious scavengers like their saltwater cousins. If you have a singing Big Mouth Billy Bass on your wall at home and have ever wondered why it doesn't look like a sea bass, now you know: it's the freshwater species. I'd never owned a Billy Bass, as I thought they were a bit naff, but I recently saw one staring at me at a car-boot sale, rather like the wild boar glug glug jugs (*see* page 185), and I just couldn't resist him. I felt sorry for him losing his home and he was just £8. Problem was, he kept going off in my bag on the way back to my car, but I couldn't turn the damn thing off, as I needed a screwdriver to remove the batteries. So I walked quickly, pretending it wasn't me. Then, would you believe it, on the way back to London, Billy started singing again – he's out of control. I can't wait to get him on the wall in my fishing room in my new house, as he's clearly a sensitive thing.

Only a couple of us were anglers, but six of us boarded the boats for a bit of alternative activity. I had bought a Tabasco Rapala® lure, which rattled, so I had to put that to good use. We caught a few bass between us. To be precise, I caught one and Matthew Fort, the food writer and journalist with whom I was travelling, said that he'd caught a few, although I'm not sure I totally believed him. But hey, it was another species under the belt and hadn't been planned among the fun and games in New Orleans.

Our fish were quite small specimens, but a year later I put my rattling lure to the test down in Cape Cod and actually caught a decent saltwater striped bass. I didn't have a landing net, but a nearby angler spotted my fish on and brought his net over. When we lifted the fish out of the water, he said that it was nice, but perhaps a little undersized. It was the biggest bass I'd ever caught – about a 5-pounder in American terms – and I was sad to have to return it. At the same time, I was impressed that their minimum catch size was so big – so my bass swam away to grow a little and be consumed by another angler later in life.

Shrimp gumbo

Serves 4–6

Gumbo is probably the best-known dish to come out of Louisiana. Over the years, I've eaten many poorly prepared gumbos with no intensity and substance, so eating a dish like this gives you a different view of it altogether. Gumbo derives its name from the word used for okra in what's now Africa's Congo. Okra is an essential ingredient for thickening this national dish. For a filé gumbo, dried and powdered sassafras leaves – from trees native to the United States – are used as a thickening agent. For you okra-haters, put off by the slimy canned variety in the local tandoori, don't worry: the okra is cooked for so long that you hardly notice it's there.

Like jambalaya, you can make this hearty gumbo soup or stew out of almost anything, and serve it as a main course or starter. It's traditionally served with cooked rice in it, but as a soup I prefer it without. A gumbo is always thickened with a roux made with oil and flour (as opposed to the butter and flour method). This might seem odd to most classically trained cooks, but it works, and in fact you wouldn't know the difference. Note that what we call prawns in the UK are referred to as shrimp by Americans.

4 tablespoons vegetable oil

3 tablespoons plain flour

1 small onion, finely chopped

1 celery stick, peeled if stringy and chopped into 1–2-cm (½–¾-inch) dice

200g (7oz) okra, trimmed and thinly sliced

1 green pepper, cored, deseeded and chopped into 1–2-cm (½–¾-inch) dice

220g (7¾oz) canned chopped tomatoes (with any large chunks chopped up)

A few splashes of Tabasco sauce

Salt and pepper

For the prawn stock:

500g (1lb 2oz) raw prawns in the shell,
    preferably with the heads on

1 tablespoon vegetable oil

1 onion, roughly chopped

3 garlic cloves, crushed

1 tablespoon tomato purée

125ml (4fl oz) white wine

10 black peppercorns

1–2 teaspoons fennel seeds

A few thyme sprigs

2 litres (3½ pints) hot fish stock (1 good-
    quality fish stock cube dissolved in that
    amount of hot water is fine)

First make the prawn stock. Remove the heads and shells from the prawns. Devein the prawns by running a knife down the back and removing the black vein, then give them a wash. Put the prawn meat in the refrigerator. Chop the heads and shells up a bit, add to a saucepan and fry in the vegetable oil on a high heat with the onion and garlic for a few minutes until they begin to colour. Add the tomato purée, white wine, peppercorns, fennel seeds, thyme and stock, bring to the boil and simmer gently for 1 hour. Remove from the heat and strain through a sieve, pushing through as much as possible with the back of a large spoon.

Meanwhile, make the roux to thicken the gumbo. Heat 3 tablespoons of the vegetable oil in a heavy-based pan and stir in the flour. Cook on a low heat for 4–5 minutes, stirring every so often, until the mixture turns a sandy colour. Remove from the heat and set aside.

Heat the remaining oil in another heavy-based saucepan and fry the onion, celery, okra and pepper for 3–4 minutes until soft. Stir in the roux and gradually add the prawn stock and canned tomatoes. Season with a little salt and pepper, add a few splashes of Tabasco sauce and simmer for 1 hour. Add the peeled prawns and cook for a further 5 minutes. Before serving, check the seasoning and add a little more Tabasco if you wish.

A boxfish on the fly out of Miami with the jeweller

Every year I go to Florida for the Art Basel Miami fair. I stay with my mate Stephen Webster, a jeweller, who has an apartment in a lovely old colonial building. It makes a great long weekend break in December, as they have warm weather there for 11 months of the year. There's the odd rainstorm at that time of year, which occasionally catches us out at the annual artists' lunch. Lots of like-minded people attend the art fair and there's always a big posse of dealers, collectors and gallery owners from London that I know, so the party and dinner invites flow and there's plenty to keep us busy for a few days.

I normally try to squeeze in a day's fishing and drag Steve along. In Miami, you can jump in an Uber and 30 minutes down the road you'll be in good fishing territory, where you can fish for all sorts (including bonefish and other species) on the good flats in Biscayne Bay.

The evening before our fishing trip we were dining in Mandolin, a very good Greek restaurant, with some art fair sponsors and a couple of girls from Quintessentially, the London-based concierge business. I asked Steve if he had all the suitable attire for fishing on the flats, like a brimmed hat and a buff to protect his neck from the sun. He obviously wasn't quite prepared. I whispered to him, 'Why don't we put the Quintessentially girls to the test and see if they can source them in the next six hours before we set off on our trip?' I've known Ben Elliot, the founder of Quintessentially, for years, as well as some of his team, but never put their services to use. Well, we put it to them and witnessed their skills in trying to give the customer just what they require. It was only a fishing hat and buff, but this wasn't the easiest ask at midnight – it would have probably been much easier to organize a chauffeur-driven Bentley for the day. We were apprehensive about whether the hat and buff would show up, but when I walked out of the lift to meet Steve in the lobby, he was standing there with a colourful fishing buff round his neck and a very smart beige fishing hat, so the girls scored ten out of ten. Steve was just as excited over the hat turning up as he was about going fishing for the day.

So we were now fully kitted up. We arrived at the quay and met Captain Bob, our fishing guide for the day. The boat trip from Key Biscayne in the Biscayne National Park conjures up some interesting historical sites of houses on stilts, 3m (10 ft) above the water, known as Stiltsville, a couple of miles out into the bay. They were built in the 1930s and earlier by people like 'Crawfish' Eddie during the Prohibition era and allegedly used for gambling, which was legal then if it took place at least a mile from shore. 'Crawfish' Eddie sold bait and beer from his shack and was known for a dish called chilau, a chowder made with crawfish that he caught under his shack. Some of the shacks were also turned into clubs, such as the Quarterdeck Club and Calvert Club. These fetched high memberships back then and were described as play palaces for lawyers, celebrities, bankers and politicians. What went on offshore can only be left to the imagination. Bob gave us the brief history on the way out, which was fascinating and not at all what we expected on the way to our bone-fishing destination.

Catching bonefish relies totally on being able to see the fish, so you can cast your fly more or less in front of their noses. It's frustrating, especially when the sun hides behind a cloud and the wind comes up, as you can't see a damn thing, even in a few feet of water. Steve and I had exactly that problem a couple of years back. We spent our day casting at nothing until I had a take, which I was convinced was a bonefish, as it took off like lightning. Well, it wasn't a bonefish, but something I'd never seen before – a boxfish. What a weird-looking thing. It looked more like a futuristic, underwater space-age vessel than a fish. I ended up catching two and releasing them. I asked Bob, our guide, if we could eat them. He said that they are delicious, one of the best-tasting fish around in the area. As he was telling me this, I caught another, double the size of the other two, so that one stayed on the boat. Bob explained the unusual bone and carcass structure of the boxfish, and that you need something serrated to get through the armoured body to access the flesh.

On returning to Steve's apartment, I had a go at filleting the boxfish, but, as Bob had explained, it had a weird, outer armoured shell that I'd never seen before. I had to use Steve's bread knife to cut through the carcass to reveal two long fillets – it was rather like a monkfish once filleted. I had to extract the fillets from the carcass by pulling them out with my hands. You learn something new every day. Steve sat at the kitchen counter fascinated and laughing at the same time, while we swigged cold beers.

That evening, we all went to a jewellery party in the Wynwood Art District. I shadowed Steve, as everyone wanted to talk jewellery and I didn't know anyone. It seemed that Steve was only interested in talking about the boxfish I'd caught. He told everyone about it and how I was going to cook it for breakfast. That fish was the talk of the town, as was how the fishing bug was gradually working on Steve.

I cooked the boxfish for breakfast the next day for Steve, his wife Asia and myself, serving it with fried plantain, corn fritters and a green tomatillo salsa – a Florida version of the classic dish I used to make at catering college called Sole Caprice (which was ironic as I ended up working there later in my career). That evening, the boxfish story continued on the Miami party scene, with more details than on the previous evening about the extreme fishy breakfast. Once again, people seemed more intrigued by Steve telling fish tales in his cockney accent.

Steve has always been fascinated by fish, even obsessive, and collects fish ornaments that he dots around the house. I've bought a few for him over the years, as it's an easy gift when you're in a bric-a-brac shop and a 1960s purple glass fish is staring at you from a pile of house clearance junk, saying, 'Find me a home.' I once bought Steve a silver octopus candelabra from the Paul Smith shop in Mayfair, London, which he was over the moon about. Fish and shellfish are often an influence in Steve's jewellery designs, and he once posed naked holding a big pollack for a charity called Fish for Love.

Steve wanted to have the launch party for one of his fish-inspired collections at HIX Oyster & Chop House, and transform the small tiled restaurant into a fish and chip shop for the evening. I decided to serve battered fish tails – mackerel tails, to be precise, as the pointed tails would hold their shape when fried and the meat would stay nice and moist. We put mackerel on the menu in two of the restaurants and saved the tails with an inch or so of flesh. We stuck the tails in the freezer until the event. They looked and tasted stunning in the little bespoke Stephen Webster-branded cones with chips and mushy peas at the bottom.

Boxfish with fried plantain, corn fritters and tomatillo salsa

Boxfish serves 4; salsa serves 6–8

You will most certainly struggle to find boxfish if you haven't caught it yourself, so try this recipe with monkfish fillets instead. You can find fresh tomatillos in some specialist greengrocer shops or in Mexican or South American shops. Tomatillo is a member of the *Physalis* (Cape gooseberry) genus, and is firm and slightly sour – which is why it's perfect for making salsa. Green or underripe tomatoes also work if you can't get hold of tomatillos. Asian supermarkets or specialist greengrocers often sell guava; if not, a pear would give a similar sweet and savoury flavour.

4 firm fish fillets, such as boxfish or
   monkfish

2 plantains or underripe bananas, peeled
   and halved lengthways

Vegetable or corn oil, for frying

1 lime, quartered, to serve

For the blackening spices:

1 teaspoon ground paprika

1 teaspoon ground thyme

1 teaspoon cayenne pepper

1 teaspoon finely ground black pepper

1 teaspoon finely ground white pepper

1 teaspoon garlic powder

For the corn fritters:

600g (1lb 5oz) cooked sweetcorn kernels,
   chopped

3 tablespoons chopped chives

1 teaspoon dried red chilli flakes

120g (4oz) gluten-free self-raising flour

About 120–150ml (4–5fl oz) scrumpy or
   dry cider

Vegetable or corn oil, for deep-frying

Sparkling water (optional)

Salt and pepper

For the tomatillo salsa:

2 tablespoons olive oil

4–5 tomatillos or 2–3 large green

    tomatoes, cut into 1-cm (½-inch) dice

3–4 guavas, cut into 1-cm (½-inch) dice, or

    2 pears, peeled, cored and diced

3 spring onions, cut in half lengthways

    and finely chopped

2 medium green chillies, finely chopped

2 tablespoons chopped fresh coriander,

    stalks and all

1 tablespoon chopped mint

Salt and pepper

To make the corn fritters, mix the sweetcorn, chives, chilli flakes and flour in a bowl, then add enough scrumpy/dry cider to make a thick batter. Season to taste with salt and pepper, mix well and leave to rest for 15 minutes. Meanwhile, preheat about 8cm (3¼ inches) of oil to 160–180°C (325–350°F) in a large, heavy-based saucepan or an electric deep-fat fryer. Drop the batter, a teaspoon at a time, into the hot fat and cook for a minute or so, or until golden, turning the fritters with a slotted spoon while they cook and removing them to drain on kitchen paper. Check the seasoning, and if the batter is a little stodgy, just let it down with some sparkling water. If you want to make the fritters in advance, cook them in a few batches without colouring them completely, then just return to the hot fat when required.

To make the salsa, mix all the ingredients together in a bowl and season to taste with salt and pepper.

Mix all the blackening spices together in a small bowl and generously coat the fish fillets. Next, get 2 frying pans, preferably nonstick. Fry the plantains/bananas in one pan with a couple of tablespoons of vegetable oil for 2–3 minutes on each side, or until golden; then keep warm. In the other pan, fry the fish for about the same amount of time, depending on the thickness of the fillets. Place the fish on warmed plates with half a plantain/banana, a spoonful or 2 of the tomatillo salsa and a wedge of lime each. Serve with the corn fritters.

A grumpy, shouty guide in Florida and deep-fried Key lime pie

A few years back, Robin Hutson and I had the urge to do a bit of saltwater fly-fishing for bonefish, because trout and salmon fishing was about as far as we'd got in our fly-fishing endeavours. Over a glass of Viña Tondonia with some Guernsey Goddess (a type of cheese, now known as Somerset Solstice) and toast off the barbecue during a riverbank lunch on the River Test, we chatted about a little bonefish trip to Florida. We found a few fishing guides in Islamorada, an hour or so down on the Florida Keys from Miami, and a hotel called the Islander Resort right across from the fishing pontoon where our guides were based. This was exciting stuff: hot weather, bonefish, tarpon and maybe permit, plus a stop-off at our mate Nick Jones's Soho Beach House in Miami en route. I'd never been there before, but Robin was involved in the build stages when he was chairman of the Soho House group after he sold Hotel du Vin.

This was before Robin and my now regular trips to the Bahamas' Andros Island (*see* page 220). I suppose we didn't really do our research properly and winged it, as it was our first stab at saltwater fly-fishing in Florida. Day one, we pre-booked a fishing guide online, and from his YouTube videos and history, he seemed like a top guide with a good catch-rate. The flats on the Florida Keys have a long history of bonefish, tarpon and permit, which are the three species that keen fly-fishermen like us regard as the Holy Grail – if you ever come across boys talking sporty fishing banter. We jumped aboard our guide's skiff, a shallow boat designed for flats fishing (this is fishing from a boat in shallow inshore waters). Of course, we started talking fishing. We soon discovered that the bones had disappeared from the Keys a couple of years ago and no one seemed to know why. The general consensus of opinion was that it was a migratory thing after a couple of heavy storms, and the bonefish hadn't returned to breed but sadly gone elsewhere. However, our guide told us there were lots of tarpon and that when the bones had been plentiful, he held – and still holds – the Florida record: a 17-pounder (that's nearly 8kg). This was a huge beast, as the average size is maybe 1.3–3kg (3lb–6lb 8oz). (In fishing terms, you'll notice that when I'm in the US, I talk pounds and ounces, and the rest is up-to-date metric.)

Fishing guides are notorious for being shouty. Our guide was not only shouty, but also grumpy and totally unhelpful in terms of guiding us and correcting our casting and other techniques – all the things you hope for when travelling such a long way and paying the same price as a business class return flight to Miami. As I've already mentiond, fishing for bonefish is all about sight fishing, which basically means you need to see the fish and know exactly where to cast your little imitation shrimp fly. These are called gotchas, Charlies, crazy ghosts and so on. You cast the fly slightly ahead of the school or single fish, then strip your line, making it bounce on the sand to imitate a distressed or feeding shrimp.

A fishing guide, who stands on a platform at the rear of the flat-bottomed skiff with a pole, will normally see the fish before you and tell you their distance. When the fish are in casting distance, he will instruct you exactly where to cast by distance and time – for example, 30m (100ft) at 10 o'clock or 15m (50 ft) at 11 o'clock. Now, if you haven't got much experience of this kind of fly-fishing, basically casting by the guide's voice alone can confuse the hell out of you, as you learned to tell the time at junior school. It's 50 years on, you are missing the fish by a few hours and being shouted at by the grumpy guide, 'Didn't you learn to tell the time? I said 10 o'clock, not 12!' The more you miss-cast, the angrier the guide gets and the more you panic and lose confidence. While you are untangling your fly line from around your neck or feet, he tells you not to bother, as we've spooked the fish off.

Well, apart from being bollocked all day long by the guide whose name I won't mention, we did see an awful lot of huge tarpon weighing over 45kg (100lb), but failed miserably to get the fly anywhere near a fish's mouth. When you're trembling with fear and trying to balance on the bow of a boat while casting a big heavy fly – bigger than bonefish flies – and this huge, missile-like fish is coming towards you, it's tough and feels as if you're freezing in an exam at school when the teacher is looking over your shoulder.

That night, Robin and I needed to let off some steam because, firstly, we hadn't caught a damn thing and, secondly, we'd been shouted at all day long. There wasn't a lot of choice along the Islamorada strip. We did, of course, find a couple of bars where we asked for recommendations from people who looked like they loved food. Of course, we desperately wanted to find the ultimate Key lime pie, as we were in that neck of the woods and every restaurant served it – and advertised the fact in the window, even if it wasn't the best pie on the Keys. I've seen all sorts of variations of this famous pie over the years and so was intrigued what we would find on its home turf.

We found a newly built restaurant that one of the barmen told us to check out. The menu looked more interesting than most and the chef even came out to see us, as he was naturally proud of his new restaurant and didn't have a clue who we were. He talked us through a few things on the menu, including what we translated as a big old pork chop, the Barnsley chop. The dish that really caught our attention, though, was the deep-fried Key lime pie! Oh yes, deep-fried like a Mars bar in batter, we were told. We chuckled, slurped more wine and obviously ordered this thing, wondering what the hell it was going to be. Well, it was a show-stopper for sure when it arrived. It was the size of the plate, but fortunately we'd decided to share it. It had every element of the Key lime pie we were looking for, including the bonus of the crisp batter encasing the zesty filling and crisp pastry. We had succeeded in our quest, and all we needed now was a fish or two to talk about instead of the deep-fried Key lime pie story.

Next day, we found a new fishing guide, Randy Towe, who was the complete opposite of the grumpy old man. He was gentle, didn't shout and actually got off his platform and gave us some tuition when we were struggling. When there is a bit of a wind up, the obvious thing is to try and cast harder, which results in your fly line going everywhere and more often than not tangling around your neck. Randy taught us to use the wind in your face to your advantage and let it help you load your back cast, which in turn sends your fly line through the air on your actual cast – sounds like common sense, but it's not until you are in Florida that someone actually tells you this.

Although we were now a bit more knowledgeable and confident, we still didn't manage to nail a tarpon. But we were somewhat wiser. On our journey back to shore, Randy's engine failed, but hey, that's boats for you. I've experienced exactly the same thing on my boat. Luckily, Randy's friend was close by, came to the rescue and towed us back in. What we did spot on our way back was Randy's name on a couple of his rods. Turns out he is a bespoke rod builder, so the least we could do was stop off at his shop once his friend had towed us back to 'sure' – no pun there, by the way, just bad luck with his surname and our trip. Robin and I bought a rod each because we didn't have a bespoke rod between us, and why wouldn't you hand the cash to the man himself?

On my return to London, I got my new toy out of its case and realized that one of the four sections was missing. How can that have happened? Anyway, I got in touch with Randy and the new one arrived. This didn't fit, so that was returned, too. I waited forever to get a new one, and when it did eventually arrive after several email reminders, it was in bits. To cut a long story short, the correct new section turned up a week before our trip to the Bahamas' Andros Island (*see* page 220), with goddamn duty to pay. The story continues with these jinxed rods, if you are wondering, and Robin's name quietly became 'Two-Tip Rob' after his rod tip actually busted with a fish on, so he had to order a new one.

The Bahamas: Andros Island

If we're lucky, Robin Hutson and I travel abroad to fish maybe once or twice a year. A few years back, we decided to extend our short Florida experience and visit Andros Island in the Bahamas. We stayed at the Andros Island Bonefish Club. This was my first visit to the Bahamas, but Robin had worked in a hotel at Nassau Beach early in his hospitality career before developing his passion for fishing. We had never really done an intense five-day fishing holiday abroad, especially for the ultimate Holy Grail, the bonefish, so this was to be a proper boys' treat to ourselves.

We found the Bonefish Club online while on the Eurostar bound for Paris for a bit of lunch. We sized up the fishing on Robin's laptop over a bottle or two of vintage Champagne and a black pudding Scotch egg I'd brought for the journey, and booked the trip immediately. This trip-to-be became the topic of our fishing chats for the months leading up to it and, of course, led to us purchasing everything we needed – or rather thought we needed – from wading boots (never used), new rods and reels, fly lines, tropical fishing sunglasses and buffs and hats to keep the reflection off while standing on the skiff. Oh, and lots of flies because everyone tells you what you need, including the guys in the tackle shops, so you have to cover all angles.

This is exactly how our fishing artillery builds up and gets a bit out of control. There's a new type of fishing in a new destination, so you need to make sure you have all the kit to do the job – oh, and maybe a new fishing travel bag for back-up rods and reels, just in case. It's not like golf, you see, where you just pick up the clubs and shoes, then pop them in the back of the car with a few extra balls in case the trees on the course get the better of you. Oh no, it's a lot more intricate than that.

In our pre-trip research, we'd discovered that the best and most economical way to get to the Bahamas was via Miami. We even found some bargain Virgin Upper Class tickets; with our air miles, it made the first leg of the trip a bit more luxurious. It's always handy to have contacts and friends of the family when you're travelling, and, of course, our mate Nick Jones has the Soho Beach House in Miami Beach, so that made a perfect stop-off point for a night or two to relax before a hard week's fishing. Obviously, we would also be able to check out what's new on the restaurant scene in Miami. You may think this is a bit of a busman's holiday, but that's what we do for a living.

We had a little arrival cocktail on the roof terrace of the Soho Beach House, and while I was waiting for Robin to unpack and come up, I clocked DJ Nick Grimshaw. I'm not sure how I recognized him, as he was lying face down on a sun lounger, so thought I'd better send him a quick text message just in case it wasn't him. Anyway, we had a beer and invited him fishing the next day. Grimmy admitted he had never fished before or even been out on a boat, so he got a quick OK from his mum who he was holidaying with and out we went.

We stopped off at an obligatory tackle shop en route to where we were getting the boat. To our disappointment, it was smaller than our rooms at the Beach House. The photography angle on the website had completely lured us in. We still managed to buy a few things that we didn't actually need, and also bought Grimmy a fancy black skull-and-cross-bone neck buff to protect him from the sun as an introductory fishing-trip gift, which he loved.

The fishing wasn't so good, but we managed to raise a sailfish up to the surface with a fly. This got our skipper excited, but that was it apart from Robin catching a little tuna, which we kept and gave to the boys in the kitchen back at the Beach House on our return. It came back from the kitchen beautifully prepared and sliced with all the sashimi accompaniments, and we sat at the bar eating the little tuna washed down with a nice ice-cold rosé. I don't think Grimmy is going to take up fishing, but at least we exposed him to it!

It takes another two short flights from Miami to reach Andros Island. The second flight is from Nassau Beach in a rickety little vintage plane. The captain holds the steps on the way up to the cabin and you have to balance each side of the plane to keep it stable while flying. If you are visiting Andros, don't expect too much unless you are fishing. It's one of those beautiful unspoiled islands with lots of half-finished buildings from the island's wealthy heyday and roads that haven't been repaired for decades. There's still a bit of a hangover from the drug-running days when little islands like Andros would have been a drop-off or hide-out point for the runners, which is not a secret. It's both interesting and a great shame to see the unattended-to buildings. But island life sees some bubbly characters and also some experienced fishing guides with lots of personality, as all they do is fish and act as one-to-one guides for clients from around the world, some with high expectations and testosterone, and some, like us, with low expectations who just want to have fun and catch the odd fish, so that we can chat about it over a few rums at the club.

After landing and a broken-down taxi ride to the Bonefish Club, we settled in at our cabin-like lodges, unpacked our kit and headed to the outside bar area where a group of Americans were drinking and laughing and talking fish. I say talking fish; it was obsessive, non-stop fishing tattle while watching the American presidential election on the TV in the clubhouse, which seemed to be on a rolling election-covering channel. The club is perfectly set up, even though it's not luxurious in any way. But we were there to fish and not lounge about in our rooms or sunbathe.

I've only caught a handful of bonefish in my life and these were all exhilarating and memorable experiences. Day one fishing on Andros, I nailed 18 fish before lunchtime. Well, I say lunchtime, it was more like frozen margarita and boat-snack time. I had to hold off cracking open our pre-mixed boat cocktail of the day, as the bones were coming in thick and fast, and there was no time for drinking on duty. The afternoon was uneventful and I only caught one fish. They were few and far between for the rest of the week too, as the sun was in and out with light winds, which meant spotting the fish was tough, even in only a few feet of water. But I'd had my fix that first morning, so I wasn't too perturbed about the lack of bonefish for the rest of the week.

On day two, Robin and I took a day off bone fishing and booked a boat to take us a few miles out into deep water for, hopefully, some bigger, more sporty species. After breakfast I told the other guests we would be cooking dinner that night and got slightly suspicious looks, as they didn't know what either of us did for a living and thought we were a pair of English jokers.

We travelled a couple of miles out beyond the shallow flats, where the water suddenly drops to a mile deep and is home to some large, interesting species like wahoo and mahi-mahi. We fished light with

heavier fly rods that we used for the bones and spinning rods. We hit into the mahi-mahi almost on arrival at our destination, and the two of us constantly had a fish on. Once you've hooked one of these amazing blue and yellow fish, they seem to attract others. The water was alive with them and they were fairly easy to hook with a fly or lure. In about three hours we had a good old haul of mahi-mahi, which is a fast-breeding fish, so there is no sustainability issue. They are also a great eating fish. We had a wahoo and Robin had a shark attack on one of his mahi. It ate a third of the fish as it got to the surface. Fair game – this often happens with fishing, as a slow-moving, distressed fish is an easy lunch for predators like shark.

In total, we had eight mahi-mahi and a wahoo in the bag. Cole, our skipper, said he would take what we didn't want to feed the local village. You see, fishing, whether you fish for sport and return the fish or catch them to eat or to feed the locals, is a great thing to do. While pulling in the fish I was carefully planning the menu for that evening. Each time Robin or I landed a fish, the menu changed somewhat and, knowing what limited ingredients they had back in the kitchen, I certainly had to think 'on the deck' a bit. I got Cole to put a few calls into his wife onshore as and when I thought up a dish. He got her picking chillies, ripe and underripe papaya, plantains and tomatoes. This was taking skippering a fishing boat and foraging to order on the end of a cell phone to a whole new level. By the time the fishing had died down and the menu was sorted in my head, we returned to the Bonefish Club. The Americans were still out bone fishing, so Robin, my kitchen bitch, and I had time to get all the fish filleted with Cole's help and prepared for the five-course meal.

Using very limited spices and ingredients, we knocked up a Sri Lankan curry with wahoo steaks cut straight through the bone, which I finished with some peanut butter off the breakfast buffet. While I was cooking the curry, Robin got to work on making some onion bahjis – he's become a real bahji expert since then.

The mahi-mahi, or dorado as it's often called, went to good use. I made sashimi with the prime parts of the loin and served this with simple slithers of chilli and soy. The other trimmings and belly were diced up to make a ceviche with the local oranges, which are quite acidic but extremely perfumed and almost lime-like. Robin made plantain crisps to serve with the ceviche. The thickest part of the fillet was marinated in the overripe, blended-up papaya with some other spices I found in the larder and then served with a green papaya and tomato salsa. I used the bones to make an Asian broth with chilli and ginger, and dropped in some nuggets of crispy fried mahi belly and tail meat.

I love cooking with minimal ingredients, and on the hoof as it were, as it really puts you to the test. I've cooked all over the world in challenging situations and tiny temporary kitchen spaces and fields, so nothing really fazes me. When there's limited cooking space and the refrigeration doesn't work, you just have to get on with it. The Americans couldn't believe the five courses we hit them with, which we'd knocked up by the time they'd got back, showered and had a refreshing post-fishing beer. Their constant fishing chit-chat turned into culinary Tourette's, with some surprise that Brits can actually cook. You see, most Americans think British food is crap and that it's all about fish and chips and roast beef. I suppose in hindsight I should have put Yorkshire puddings on the table with some sauceboats of gravy to see their reactions, then pulled out the real food.

A couple of the Americans were independent – from the group that is, not politically – and asked when we were returning the following year so that they could book their slot. We certainly did return the following year with some pals and recreated the feast with a couple of different species, including a shark that was determined to eat our fish before we did – so we did the deed and cooked him for supper.

Mahi-mahi sashimi

Serves 4

When you have fish that's only been out of the water for a few hours, you don't need to cook it. This is especially true of a fish like mahi-mahi. On my trip to Andros Island, it made a great appetizer for our new fishing-lodge friends. Luckily, I had packed soy sauce and ponzu, so I had all the ingredients I needed, apart from some goat chillies which are grown on the island.

400g (14oz) skinless very fresh firm-fleshed white fish fillet

1 chilli, very thinly sliced
Good quality soy sauce or ponzu, to serve

With a sharp knife, slice the raw fish as thinly as possible and arrange on the serving plates. Put a slice of chilli on each and serve with the soy sauce or ponzu.

Andros Island fish curry

Serves 4

We kept one of the wahoo we'd caught because, while the thing was fighting, I'd thought this boy was going to be curry if I manage to land him. On a remote island, you have to make do with what you've got, and while we didn't have the full larder of spices I would have liked, there was enough to hand to give the curry a bit of a kick, mellowed down with some peanut butter. I find that a fish curry always works best when served on the bone, and the long, slender, firm-fleshed body of a wahoo is perfect for this. Back home, you could use all sorts of other fish, including huss, monkfish or even a good-sized trout (if you don't mind tackling the bones).

1.5kg (3lb 5oz) fish on the bone, cut into 3-cm (1¼-inch) -thick slices

60g (2¼oz) ghee or vegetable oil

3 medium onions, roughly chopped

5 large garlic cloves, crushed

1 tablespoon grated fresh root ginger

3 small, medium-strength chillies, deseeded and finely chopped

1 teaspoon cumin seeds

2 teaspoons ground cumin

1 teaspoon mustard seeds (black or yellow)

½ teaspoon fenugreek seeds

1 teaspoon cumin powder

Pinch of saffron threads

1 teaspoon freshly grated turmeric root or 1 teaspoon ground turmeric

Good pinch of curry leaves

½ teaspoon ground paprika

1 teaspoon fennel seeds

2 teaspoons tomato purée

1.3 litres (2¼ pints) hot fish stock (1 good-quality fish stock cube dissolved in that amount of hot water is fine)

2 tablespoons peanut butter

3 tablespoons chopped fresh coriander leaves

Salt and pepper

Basmati rice, to serve

Season the pieces of fish to taste with salt and pepper. Heat half the ghee/oil in a large, heavy-based saucepan and fry the fish on a high heat until lightly coloured. Remove the fish with a slotted spoon and put to one side. Add the remainder of the ghee/oil to the pan and fry the onions, garlic, ginger and chillies for a few minutes until they begin to soften. Add the rest of the spices and continue cooking for a couple of minutes with the lid on to release the flavours, stirring every so often.

Add the tomato purée and stock, bring to the boil, season to taste again and simmer for 45 minutes. Take a cupful of the sauce, blend in a blender until smooth and pour back into the pan. Add the peanut butter and stir until melted in, then add the pieces of fish and simmer for 15 minutes. Add the coriander and simmer for a further 5 minutes, seasoning again if necessary. Serve with the basmati rice.

Macho margarita

Makes 1

This cocktail was created in 2008 by Adrian Hernandez at Colibrí, a Mexican bistro in San Francisco.

500ml (18fl oz) agave nectar

250ml (9fl oz) hot water

2 pickled guindilla chilli peppers

1 teaspoon Wray & Nephew White Overproof Rum

2 teaspoons Edmond Briottet Curaçao Triple Sec Liqueur

35ml (1fl oz) lime juice

20ml (¾fl oz) agave water

50ml (2fl oz) Calle 23 Blanco tequila

Ice cubes

Pour the agave nectar and hot (but not boiling) measured water into a jug or bowl and mix. Chop the pickled peppers into small pieces, keeping a 4-cm (1½-inch) piece with the stalk attached for a garnish. This should be sliced down the middle, so that it can rest on the edge of the glass. Place the remaining peppers on a side plate with the rum and the liqueur, and ignite with a lighter. While the peppers are burning, pour the lime juice, agave water and tequila into the smaller half of a cocktail shaker. Extinguish the flaming peppers and transfer them to the smaller half of the shaker. Fill the larger half of the shaker with ice cubes and join the 2 halves together. Shake for 15–20 seconds until you have your desired dilution and the cocktail is nicely chilled. Strain the cocktail into a chilled coupe glass and garnish with the piece of pepper.

Costa Rica: Crocodile Bay ceviche and sailfish

Years ago, back in 2002, I went on a trip to Costa Rica with my old friend Rory Ross, a journalist. He was writing a travel piece for the *Independent*. I had a long-standing Saturday cookery column with the newspaper; for once, I didn't have to write the column. My fishing friends always banged on about catching sailfish on the fly during trips to Dubai. I'd never quite managed to fit a visit into my schedule, but was itching to have a go at catching sailfish. As you can imagine, catching a big-game fish like this is quite a feat on a light fly rod, as they can grow to 50kg (110lb) or more. After all the talk, we checked out catching sailfish on the fly in Costa Rica – there had to be something on my fishing list I could cross off. We found a place called Crocodile Bay in Corcovado National Park in the jungly southwest of the country, where we were able to fish for sailfish on the fly. Although the season wasn't in full swing, you never know and it was definitely worth a go.

Prior to our visit to Crocodile Bay, I wanted to check out some authentic ceviche, as most restaurants in the UK serve ceviche sort of sliced up, a bit like Japanese sashimi. I knew this was a bastardized version of the real deal. We went to several restaurants with the owner of El Pelícano in Playa Herradura, and tried ceviche in various forms, which I knew we could improve on. Some of the places were using marlin, which isn't on my PC fish-to-use list. Although we were going to fish for its cousin, the sailfish, the following day, this would be on a sustainable catch-and-release basis. You see, some fishermen catch tuna and swordfish in their nets, along with other billfish like sails and marlin. As the name suggests, billfish are a group of predatory fish with prominent bills. Some fisheries are far better than others at reducing the capture of non-target species, known as by-catch in the trade, but by the time the fish are filleted and chopped up, it's difficult to tell the difference. Not all fish are sustainable and I personally feel that all billfish should be returned.

We did stumble across a fairly rough-looking restaurant on the beach. I always love looking at other people's food before I order, so I peeped over a few diners' shoulders to see what they were eating. I clocked what looked like a ceviche and ordered it, making sure first that it wasn't made with any chopped-up billfish. It was parrotfish that had been caught by a local. These fish have beautiful colours when fresh out of the water and taste delicious, so good on them. The ceviche was a slightly

231

fruity, sweet-and-sour concoction containing a papaya purée with some lime juice and the usual chilli, onion and coriander. Interestingly, it was served with plantain and cassava chips to mop up the ceviche. Since my introduction to authentic ceviche, I've often served it with plantain and cassava, as these are readily available in London, albeit imported. I've even used vegetables such as beetroot and parsnips, which are home grown.

I suppose the thing I learned about ceviche is that there are lots of variations depending on what you have at hand, what's in season and what country you're in. You also don't need to use prime fish, as the second-division fish such as pouting, whiting and mackerel that we have in the UK make a ceviche that's just as good as one made with a prime fish like sea bass.

What I've also learned about ceviche is that it can match strong alcohol. In Costa Rica, we washed the ceviche down with guaro, a local rum. Since then I've matched it with tequila in Mexico, rum in Guyana in South America and Black Cow vodka and gin in the UK. I suppose the delicate yet punchy ceviche spices work hand in hand with pure hard liquor. I've even done interesting cocktails to go with ceviche and raw-fish concoctions. For a particular dinner in Malibu, I served raw spot prawns (which look like tiny lobsters) with a stock made from their shells turned into a chilled, spiced-up version of the classic bullshot, which is usually made with vodka and beef stock. This worked a treat and fulfilled my passion for utilizing everything.

Shell Shot

Makes 8

I've made bullshot with beef stock and duck shot with wild duck stock to take shooting or fishing. This is a fishy version using lobster or prawn shells. You can also use crayfish or crab shells. Once you've made the stock, freeze it in usable quantities so that you can take it fishing, then simply add the vodka and other ingredients when you heat up the stock.

For the broth:

1 or 2 lobster or prawn shells, chopped and rinsed under a cold tap

2 litres (3½ pints) hot fish stock (3 good-quality fish stock cubes dissolved in that amount of hot water is fine)

1 small onion, roughly chopped

2 garlic cloves, halved

1 small leek, trimmed, cleaned and roughly chopped

2 celery sticks, roughly chopped

½ tablespoon tomato purée

1 bay leaf

2 thyme sprigs

2 tablespoons fennel seeds

1 teaspoon black peppercorns

Salt and pepper

To serve:

100–200ml (3½–7fl oz) vodka, depending on the occasion

½ tablespoon Worcestershire sauce

2 good pinches of celery salt

Tabasco sauce

Put all the ingredients for the broth in a saucepan, bring to the boil and simmer very gently for 45 minutes, skimming off any scum as it accumulates on the surface. Strain the broth through a fine-meshed sieve into a clean saucepan, then season with salt and pepper. Add all the serving ingredients to taste (the quantities listed above are only a guide), bring back to the boil and pour into a vacuum flask ready for your trip.

* * *

Back to the fishing. I hadn't looked forward to a day's fishing like this quite so much before – and that was without even knowing if we were guaranteed to catch anything, as it was out of season. When we rocked up at Crocodile Bay, it was not at all what I 'd expected – whatever that was! Our rooms were lodges that surrounded the main fishing lodge and bar. On the way to my lodge, a crocodile popped his head out of the water in a pond right outside of my room. 'Don't worry,' said the member of staff carrying my bags, 'We have jaguars, too!'

We met the Director of Fishing, Todd Staley, a wily sea dog from Florida, in the fishing and souvenir shop. Todd was to be our captain the next day and talked us through the usual seafaring stuff. Todd was already geared up for sail on the fly with 14-weight fly rods and surface popper flies the size of a baby chicken. He explained what was going to happen if and when we spotted a sailfish on the surface. Rubber squid lures without hooks, known as teasers, would be trolled off the back of the boat to attract the sailfish. Trolling is a fishing technique in which one or more fishing lines, with lures or bait, are drawn through the water (often imitating a distressed fish).

Todd stripped off 10m (33ft) or so of my fly line with the surface popper into a bucket at the stern of the boat. 'Be ready to toss that fly into the wake of the boat when I yell and the drag is all set,' he said. OK, we would see what happened. We trolled around at about 10 knots for a couple of hours while listening to Todd's stories. He's tackled every species of sporting fish, and most types of sporting fishermen. 'If the fish bite, everything's fine,' he said. 'If they don't, suddenly the ceiling fans are squeaky and the loos don't flush fast enough.' Todd kept us captivated with his tales of the ocean and how he'd skippered for the novelist Ernest Hemingway. We had no choice but to listen, as there was nothing happening behind the stern of the boat.

Just as I had almost given up even sighting a fin chasing the teasers, Todd yelled, 'SAIL! Toss that fly in the wake, Mark.' Right, OK, here we go then, I thought. Todd and his deckhand reeled in the teasers. Then I spotted the large dorsal fin of a sailfish chasing the teasers. The fish turned his head and grabbed my popper. Everything seemed to go into slow motion, but then it all speeded up and all I could feel was my reel spinning and my rod bending with no sign of the fish.

'Keep your hand off the spool!' Todd yelled. Yes, shit, I didn't know what I was doing – it wasn't a trout; it was something that felt like it wasn't in my control. I saw this fish leap out of the water some 200m (650ft) away. 'Is that my fish, Todd?' I asked. 'Yes, keep the line tight, Mark, and don't let his head turn away from you.' Jesus, this was turning into a fast-thinking, outer-body experience: I was trying to listen to Todd, keep hold of the rod and not let the fish turn his head, while pulling the rod towards me and reeling in when I could. 'Mark, remember your leader is only 20 pounds and that fish is 80 pounds plus, but you're doing well, good fishing.' I hadn't trembled and been under so much pressure in my life, and was trying to work out how the hell I was going to get this fish anywhere near the boat, let alone onboard.

After 30 minutes, it became a war of who was the strongest: me or the goddamn fish. The sea was a bit choppy and the boat was rocking around. I was holding on to just a heavyweight single-handed fly rod and trying to control this wild thing on the end of my line. Time passed as if I were dreaming and every muscle in my body was aching, but I couldn't let this fish turn his head and snap the bloody 20-pound leader that Todd kept conveniently reminding me about. Todd became the physiotherapist guiding me through the now 45-minute battle. 'OK, he's gone under the boat now, keep your rod tip high so I can see him,' Todd yelled. I got a glimpse of the sailfish just below the surface. 'Reel in a bit and lift the rod tip up.' The deckhand grabbed my leader and caught hold of the huge fin and tail at the same time. Then the fish was on the boat before I could say, 'Oh shit!' Todd said, 'OK, quick, let's get a photo of him on your lap and then we'll release him.' This all seemed to happen in a matter of seconds.

After a shake of slimy hands and a pat on the back from everyone, a cold beer was shoved into my hand. 'That was a good fish, Mark, and well handled – you nailed him.' I didn't really have a clue what I was doing. It was rather like trout fishing, but scary and on a large scale. We trolled those teasers round for another hour, but the sea was getting angrier and so we headed back to shore.

That trip took our usual fly-fishing to a completely different level. 'Let's go to the bar!' yelled Todd. There were some American anglers at the bar, talking fishing. 'How did you do, guys?' they asked. I was still a bit wobbly at this point, but said, 'A sail.' 'Wow, good stuff,' a voice from behind a glass of bourbon on the rocks yelled. 'On the fly,' I added. Their heads turned. 'On the fly, are you kiddin' us?' 'Oh no, an 85-pounder on the fly, guys,' I answered. 'You Brits deserve a drink then – more bourbon please, and one for Captain Todd Staley.' Glasses clinked and a sense of achievement rattled through my body, which was numbed after a few more celebratory bourbons.

Australia: A whistle-stop tour

My very good friend and wine supplier John Hutton has taken us on some amazing wine trips worldwide over the years. The one to beat them all some 14 years ago was a trip to Sydney followed by Queensland in New Zealand (*see* page 241). It was a proper whistle-stop tour to the point where we didn't unpack our suitcases over the two weeks. It was 2011 and my book *Fish etc.* had just been published. I did a book-launch dinner at Nigel Lacy's Bayswater Brasserie in Sydney, to coincide with our wine trip, so invited a few people I knew there, including my very close late friend and chef Jeremy Strode. I'd worked with Jeremy when I first moved to London at the Grosvenor House hotel in Park Lane. He had a restaurant called Bistrode in an old butcher's shop in Surry Hills, a suburb of Sydney, and was often referred to as St John of Sydney. I went there several times on my visits to Australia. He sadly took his life in 2017, but was there to enjoy the fun at the time and on many occasions after that.

The day after the book-launch dinner, we went out on a boat with George Kerr, which was one of the other highlights of our visit to Sydney. We were introduced by John Susman, who I'd met several times in London and is an iconic figure in the fish business over there. He once called me out of the blue when I was working at the Caprice Group to introduce himself. He asked if I fancied having a look at some sustainable lobster, the clawless variety called crawfish or, confusingly, crayfish in some parts of the world. I agreed and he said that he would send some over. A week later, a polystyrene box the size of a coffin turned up. On opening the lid, I found a dozen or so live lobsters packed in straw, as lively as if they had just come out of the water. Rather than stick them on the restaurant menu, I invited some friends in the business round to my flat in Great Eastern Street for a crawfish supper. I used to host spontaneous refrigerator-clearing suppers, utilizing ingredients and dishes left over from photoshoots for the *Independent* magazine, as it was a great way to use stuff up and have a last-minute dinner party.

The crawfish night got some good responses, and about ten of us ate grilled and boiled crawfish with different sauces and dressings, all washed down with several magnums of wine. Unfortunately, my flat stank of grilled lobster for weeks and I went through a lot of joss sticks and scented candles to get rid of the lingering aroma. You can catch the occasional crawfish in British waters, but they are rare and in my opinion should be returned, unlike in most other countries where they are as common as our lobsters.

George was also a good mate of Nigel Lacy's and a partner in the renowned wine producer Amisfield, which makes a great Pinor Noir, although we didn't realize this until we were on the boat. The boat trip was pure pleasure, even though I did only have my travel fishing rod with me, which I cast about six times into the calm water. Onboard, the wine tasting distracted me from the fishing somewhat. Wherever I am in the world, with rod in hand, I give it everything I've got. So, now and then, I'd break away from the wine tasting and get casting again into the glassy blue water. I was quite surprised to have no interest whatsoever, even though I used almost every fly and lure in my box – but nothing. Maybe some larger predators were lurking below the boat, which is often the case when there's no fish, or maybe it was just one of those days when you blank.

The other distraction was lunch, which consisted of wok-fried native mud crabs, prepared for us by the chef back at the Bayswater Brasserie and wrapped in foil to keep hot for our boat lunch. We also had some fantastic wines, as you can imagine. This was a great way to do a hot crab dish. I have used it many times back in Dorset, using our native brown crabs or even lobster, in exactly the same way when I've pulled my lobster pots and had my friends round for supper. We also had some freshly boiled Morton Bay bugs, which are alien-looking crustaceans like nothing you will have seen or eaten before. The flesh is sort of sweet and lobster-like, but delicious with some spiced-up, thick mayonnaise and washed down with high-end Champagne – I only wish I could remember what this was!

That evening, after a long, luxurious, merry and educational session on the boat, we met Cameron and Allister Ashmead from Elderton Wines, one of the most highly regarded wine producers in Australia. They took us to the famous Rockpool restaurant, owned by Neil Perry.

From the minute we arrived and sat down, the sommelier watched us like a hawk. The two wine boys were gods in the eyes of this young and enthusiastic sommelier, as they are to those in the wine world in general. I sat next to Cameron, ploughing through the eight-course dinner that had been prepared for us. Halfway through, I asked him if he'd be able to tell the difference between the three vintages of Semillon we had lined up in front of us if I shuffled them around. Anyway, I did just that, as the sommelier looked on with focused eyes and seeming somewhat confused.

Cameron downed three half glasses in a row without taking a breath. The sommelier looked at us in horror. Cameron shook his head and said, 'No!' He put his hand up to the sommelier and said, 'Six bottles of Beck's please.' A classic merry day off the water, never to be forgotten and a story to always tell at the right moment.

Wok-fried crab

Serves 4

I have made this dish several times at home with the British native brown crab. I've even made it with lobster on the odd occasion when the haul outweighed that of the crab. Some people are a bit put off by the shells, but a dish like this is pure spicy indulgence, and you can't possibly not get stuck in with your hands and get messy.

1 live crab, weighing about 1–1.5kg (2lb 4oz–3lb 5oz)

Vegetable oil, for deep-frying

2 tablespoons sesame oil

1 teaspoon ground black pepper

1 teaspoon ground white pepper

2 teaspoons ground cumin

2 star anise, coarsely ground

1 teaspoon ground cinnamon

2 tablespoons sea salt

Juice of 2 limes

8 snake beans (yardlong beans) or 150g (5½oz) prepared green beans, cooked in salted boiling water for 4–5 minutes and drained

Handful of coriander leaves, to garnish

Place the crab in a large saucepan of salted water, bring to the boil and simmer for 2 minutes. Drain the crab and run it under a cold tap for 4–5 minutes to cool. Remove the outer main shell and discard or save this to make a soup or sauce. Remove the large claws and just crack them on the main piece of the claw at both joints, keeping the claws intact. Remove the dead man's fingers and chop the main body in half.

Preheat about 8cm (3¼ inches) of oil to 140–150°C (275–300°F) in a large, heavy-based saucepan or an electric deep-fat fryer. Cook the pieces of crab in the hot fat in a couple of batches for 3–4 minutes, then remove with a slotted spoon and drain on kitchen paper. Chop the 2 pieces of body in half again.

Meanwhile, heat 2 tablespoons of the frying oil and the sesame oil in a wok and gently fry all the spices and salt for 1 minute. Add the pieces of crab and continue cooking in the wok for 4–5 minutes, turning every so often. Add the lime juice, stir well on a high heat, then toss in the beans. Transfer to a serving dish and scatter with the coriander.

New Zealand: A whirlwind wine tour and blue cod on Milford Sound

My first trip to New Zealand, and the last one I may add, was a bit of a whistle-stop wine trip after Australia with John Hutton. Our first port of call was the Alana Estate Vineyard in Martinborough, and then we went down to the Dog Point Vineyard in Blenheim. Ivan Sutherland and James Healy used to run Cloudy Bay before starting up together on a smaller scale with Dog Point – and this vineyard has certainly been a coup for the NZ wine industry.

Next stop was the Isabel Estate in Marlborough, where we had a great New Zealand-style barbecue, the highlight of which was a delicious dish of whitebait patties. Whitebait varies around the world, but the word generally refers to small fish. These little fish weren't whitebait as I know them, but looked more like elvers, the little seasonal matchstick-like eels that make an annual journey from the Sargasso Sea to Europe on the Gulf Stream, usually arriving in rivers in South West England and Wales (*see* page 76 for more on elvers).

In the UK, elvers, which are also known as glass eels, are hellishly expensive and generally cost about £300-plus a kilo. Well, these New Zealand lookalikes certainly didn't cost that kind of money and seemed more like the price we pay for whitebait, which isn't that much at all. The 'whitebait' were simply mixed into a light batter, pan-fried like blinis until crisp and then served with a caper mayonnaise. They were absolutely delicious. I couldn't even contemplate serving this dish using elvers, as the crisp, blini-like patties would be the price of caviar.

On the back of the boat trip in Sydney with George, we made a minor detour to Amisfield in Central Otago to check out the winery and the cellar door, which in Antipodean terms is the name for a restaurant, tasting rooms and/or shop in a winery. The best restaurant food we ate in New Zealand was actually at Amisfield. The chef certainly understood what simple Italian food was all about and how it should be executed to retain freshness and flavour.

We also visited Greg Hay, then owner of the fantastic Peregrine Wines, which is one of the best vineyards in the mainly Pinot Noir-producing area of Central Otago. Like a lot of Antipodean wineries, there is also something else on offer other than the wine production and guided tours. Greg created a fantastic landscaped winery, which he used for concerts and all sorts of other events. This attracted people to the winery who wouldn't normally visit.

Greg took us in his friend's helicopter over the snow-capped mountains to the Milford Sound fjord where he keeps his boat.

Helicopter is the only way you can reach this remote spot, unless you fancy driving for 12 hours. It was one of those random surprise trips where we didn't know quite what was in store, except being told to bring our travel rods. I take at least one travel rod with me wherever I go, even if it's not a fishing trip, because, as on this occasion, you never know where you're going to end up. I never want to miss a fishing opportunity, so the rods and a few flies and lures always have a place in my suitcase.

When we arrived at Milford Sound, we set off up the fjord in the boat with Greg's partner, Derek Brown, then anchored in a sheltered spot. Derek dived for scallops, giant mussels and rock lobster, their native clawless species. This is sometimes called crawfish or crayfish, which is confusing because we know crayfish as a freshwater species.

While Derek was down on the bottom, we jigged for blue cod and caught more than enough for lunch. This was a first for me in New Zealand, and the first time fishing for blue cod, which is not very common in the UK where it is known as sablefish. I've never seen or caught it in our waters. I caught more than enough blue cod for lunch. Of course, I'd already organized the ingredients in advance to make some sashimi and a ceviche, which is a must wherever you are in the world. The blue cod weren't that big, but still put up a very good fight on light tackle and so deserved a good place at the cabin table.

The boat was well equipped and had a barbecue onboard, as you would expect. We grilled the lobster and scallops on the barbecue and consumed some of Greg's Pinot Noir, which John taught us should be served slightly chilled. This isn't very traditional in Central Otago, but John certainly convinced Greg that this was the way forward. We chilled the wine over the side of the boat in Greg's diving nets, which were emptied of the lobsters and scallops, while I prepared lunch. I incorporated some raw lobster into the ceviche and sashimi, which I served in the scallop shells.

Whitebait patties

Serves 4–6

The word whitebait is used worldwide for various types of small fish – but the shape and taste obviously differ depending on the species. The ones we had in New Zealand resembled elvers, although getting hold of these might prove tricky. Apart from our own species of whitebait, I have come across tiny, eel-like fish in Taj Stores in Brick Lane in London, but it's up to you what form of whitebait you use.

1 egg, beaten

80–100g (3–3½oz) self-raising flour

A little milk, to mix

150–200g (5½–7oz) whitebait or elvers

Vegetable oil, for frying

Salt and cayenne pepper

To serve:

Lemon wedges

Tartare sauce or mayonnaise mixed with capers, chilli and parsley

Whisk the egg, flour and milk together to form a smooth batter, then season to taste with salt and cayenne pepper. Mix the batter and whitebait together. Heat a little vegetable oil in a large frying pan. Drop tablespoonfuls of the mixture into the pan and cook for 2 minutes on each side until the whitebait are crisp. Repeat with the remainder of the mixture, keeping the cooked whitebait warm. Serve with lemon wedges and tartare sauce or the caper mayonnaise.

South Africa:
A tuna frenzy in Margate

I'm not talking Margate in Kent here – this was about 20 years ago when I visited my friend Mark Burnett for a New Year's holiday. As in North America, in South Africa they named a lot of their coastal towns after British ones. This Margate was just outside Johannesburg on the KwaZulu-Natal south coast, and where Mark had a seaside residence, which we used as our New Year's holiday retreat.

As beautiful as it is in South Africa, back then it was still a little, well, wild. On our first day, one of the guests had all his clothes stolen through a slightly open window – someone had used a fishing rod to lift the clothes one by one from an open suitcase while we were on the beach. As I said, my fishing kit goes wherever I travel, so luckily that wasn't stolen from my bedroom – unless they used my rod to nick the other guest's clothes and kindly returned it afterwards, but I doubt that.

I have the urge to fish wherever I am, so Mark fixed up an offshore fishing trip with a local skipper for us. Having said that, it wasn't that far offshore, only a reef just 3km (2 miles) out where we fished for bonito and white tuna. The reef was alive with fish and we started catching immediately, trolling lures up and down the reef. We had one hell of a day on light tackle, landing a fish almost every ten minutes until the last half hour when I had a good-sized tuna on. But it stopped fighting and the line went slack. Two sharks appeared from below the boat, and that fast, fighting tuna was no more. The water turned red – just as it does in a shark movie – and the sharks enjoyed the easy lunch I'd provided. They even took half of my Rapala® lure while they chopped away at the tuna right in front of our eyes. Oh well, that's fishing, and the tuna put up a good fight. In these waters you always have to look out for predators, whatever you are fishing for. With one nice-sized fish down, there was certainly plenty of fish for everyone, and a slow-moving tuna that's been hooked doesn't stand a chance.

The skipper said that we'd been lucky, as he's usually plagued all day by sharks just sitting under the boat waiting for an easy lunch from anglers. This had apparently never been an issue until the reef became popular for fishing. I couldn't complain, as we had about 15 fish in total. While we were catching, I'd asked Mark if we should cook up a tuna frenzy for a New Year's Eve supper. His eyes lit up and he said that there was the same number of dinner guests as fish, so there was plenty to go around, for sure.

Luckily, we hadn't shopped for the big dinner yet and now there was no need to buy any protein with our haul. All I needed was some Asian ingredients because I was planning to keep the dishes as simple and clean as possible – maybe just a couple of cooked dishes and the rest raw. The shopping back then was a lot harder than the fishing in that part of South Africa, which makes a change, as it's usually the fish that are the challenging bit. I more or less found what I needed and improvised by using ground-up fresh root ginger instead of wasabi, which actually worked really well and did the job of pickled ginger and wasabi all in one.

Sashimi and sushi, tataki and ceviche were certainly going on the menu, along with steaks grilled on the barbecue, or *braai* as they call it in South Africa, served with some locally inspired salsas. It took me a good few hours to get all the tuna prepared into the various cuts, including prime top loin and belly. The housekeepers welcomed the stuff we weren't going to use with open arms to feed their families. The pre-cooking or 'not cooking' is the messy bit, but also rewarding post-fishing as you can eat your catch and make your guests very happy.

I was foraging on the beach for more wild seashore ingredients and perhaps some driftwood or large leaves to use as serving platters – just to up the natural presentation – and in the distance in the wash of the sea I spotted a telegraph post covered with something. On closer inspection, I found that it was full of goose barnacles, which are known as *percebes* in Spain. These are a highly prized seafood delicacy, like little jewel-like claws, and contain a succulent piece of gelatinous meat once lightly cooked.

They must have travelled a fair way, I thought, and be dead. However, I then saw they were all still alive. This was an unusual, amazing and luxurious find because they would have been living on the piece of driftwood for months or more from wherever they started their journey. What a surprise addition to our New Year's Eve grand buffet. Apart from me, no one had ever seen them before, let alone eaten them. It took a bit of persuading, as all the guests were a bit suspicious, but eventually everyone tucked in with some homemade mayonnaise and shared the extra free luxury ingredient.

Bonito three ways

Once you have prepared your carefully caught tuna and cut out the prime eye of meat for the dishes opposite and overleaf, you'll be left with the fatty belly, which is a highly prized Japanese cut. You then have some thinner tail bits and some trim, which can all be used for the tartare recipe. If you want to push the boat out, make a stock by blanching the bones and simmering it for 30 minutes or so, then use this for a fragrant Asian broth.

Spicy tuna belly tartare

Serves 4

This recipe uses dashi, which is a clear stock made from dried fish and kelp, to which you add the fatty belly and other trim from the tuna.

150g (5½oz) yellowfin tuna or bonito belly

120ml (4fl oz) cold dashi

1 teaspoon finely grated fresh root ginger

1 small, medium-strength chilli, finely
  chopped

½ tablespoon chopped chives

Salt

2 large radishes, thinly sliced and finely
  shredded, to garnish

Finely chop the tuna/bonito belly and season to taste with salt. Mix the cold dashi with the ginger, chilli and half the chopped chives, pour into 4 small chilled soup bowls or Asian bowls. Mould the fish into 4 rounds using a pastry cutter or cup and place one in the centre of each bowl. Arrange the radishes on top and sprinkle with the remaining chopped chives.

Tataki of tuna with carrot salad

Serves 4, as a starter

With tataki, although the tuna is barely cooked, it takes on quite a different identity to that of raw fish. It can be served with accompaniments that you wouldn't normally have with a typical sashimi. You see beef and tuna tataki on restaurant menus in Japanese restaurants, but it's traditionally a peasant dish and generally served at home. Lucky peasants, I say.

400g (14oz) sashimi-quality, centre-cut yellowfin tuna or bonito fillet, fully trimmed and skinned

1 tablespoon sweet or thick soy sauce, plus extra for serving

2 teaspoons sesame oil

2 large carrots, finely shredded on a mandolin or by hand

1 spring onion, finely diced

Small piece of fresh root ginger (about 10g/¼oz), scraped and finely chopped or grated

1 tablespoon rice wine vinegar

1 tablespoon chopped fresh coriander

Salt and pepper

Cut the piece of tuna/bonito into 4 lengthways so that you have rough cylinder shapes. Roll the pieces in the soy sauce, removing any excess. Heat the sesame oil in a heavy-based frying pan until it's almost smoking, then cook the fish for literally 10 seconds on each side and remove from the pan. Mix the carrots with the spring onion, ginger, rice vinegar and coriander, and season to taste with salt and pepper. Arrange the carrots on 4 serving dishes, then cut each piece of fish into 4 or 5 slices with a sharp knife. Arrange the fish on top of the carrots and serve with extra soy sauce.

Sashimi with hot soy and ginger dressing

Serves 4

Sashimi can be made with other fish such as tuna, mackerel, sea bass or scallops, but make sure that it is as fresh as possible, preferably no more than a day old.

300–400g (10½–14oz) centre-cut yellowfin tuna or bonito fillet, fully trimmed and skinned

3 tablespoons light soy sauce

3 tablespoons mirin

3 tablespoons sesame oil

30g (1oz) fresh root ginger, scraped and thinly sliced

4 garlic cloves, thinly sliced

Slice the tuna/bonito fillet thinly and arrange directly on the serving plates. Put the soy, mirin, sesame oil, ginger and garlic in a small saucepan and bring to the boil. Spoon the hot dressing over the tuna/bonito slices and serve immediately.

Tokyo

Twenty-odd years ago, I was invited to Tokyo to cook for a week at the Park Hyatt hotel where the film *Lost in Translation* was set and filmed. In fact, I cooked there two years in a row. The brief was to create a typically British menu in the European brasserie restaurant. It was so long ago now that I can only just about remember the dishes, but braised beef in Guinness was certainly on there, as was bread and butter pudding, potted shrimps and a few other classics that would appear on the menus at The Ivy and Le Caprice. I sent recipes with photos ahead of time, and when I turned up at the hotel, there was the late Adrian Gill, with whom I had just done The Ivy and Caprice books, and a few of those dishes were on the menu. Sadly, Adrian was leaving for the UK, but said that Paul Smith was still knocking around. Judging by our welcome reception at the airport and hotel, I realized just how much they love British culture and food.

When I arrived in the kitchen, there were about ten chefs with the whole menu plated up for me, with some dishes having options A, B and C with different cuts for me to choose such as the braised beef. Those guys were so organized. Day one of the menu, I went to tweak a dish a little and the head chef said that this would put the guys in a spin, so I left it and for the week every dish was 100 per cent consistent, like clockwork, so I could see why he'd asked me to hold off.

Tokyo was certainly fun. Every night at 9.30pm on the dot we would be escorted out to dinner. Our first meal was at a tiny ten-seater restaurant called Asakusa Sushi Ken. The first dish was dancing prawns served by Amen. This is basically live prawns lifted out of the tank with a butterfly net and carefully peeled in front of you, so you end up with four wriggling prawns on your plate, with freshly squeezed yuzu juice as well, if you wish. Quite delicious they were, too. Then the minute you're finished, the shells are returned and served crispy fried with Maldon sea salt crunched over them. This experience has stuck in my head and culinary bible, and when we get local Lyme Bay prawns, I do the same with the shells – but obviously not the live wriggling flesh, as that probably wouldn't go down at all well in the UK.

This was my first taste of Tokyo. Every day I ate authentic Japanese food after our evening service, which gradually changed my perception of what I had been eating in London all these years. I took one of my young protégés, Lee Streeton, with me and after our first taste of Tokyo we thought we should check out what happened after midnight. We weren't that adventurous, but ended up in a huge bar that seemed to be full of American military and young Japanese girls. Towards the end of the night, I lost Lee and couldn't find him anywhere.

For some reason, although we were in a new city, I'd thought he would be safe, so I headed back to the hotel thinking that he had done the same thing. I turned up for duty the following morning and Lee appeared a little later, looking a bit the worse for wear. When I asked where he'd gone, he replied, 'Nowhere, I woke up with my head on the bar and everyone had gone.' I won't recount what happened every night, but we did have a few late nights. The first night we told the doorman and concierge that we'd been to the fish market, which I don't think convinced them, but the day we did actually go to the fish market, they smiled and said, 'Fish market?' Well, yes, again.

Every night, after service, we were taken to small, interesting restaurants, which were all fantastic. On the third evening, we went to a place in a basement. I wish I could remember its name: we sat at the bar and the kitchen was basically a four-ring burner with a few pots simmering away. The chef started chatting to us as he dissected a huge metre-long garfish. He cut it meticulously into sashimi slices, which were served with the best soy I'd ever tasted.

When we'd finished the garfish, the chef brought out a polystyrene box from the refrigerator containing wild river turtles – we'd never seen those before, but we were in Japan. The minute he opened the lid, the tortoise-sized turtles started running wild all over the kitchen. The simmering pots at the back of the stove were where the turtles ended up. I'm not sure to this day what the liquid in the pots was, but within an hour we were served a broth with chunks of the turtles. What an interesting flavour, and not what I had expected at all. I'm not quite sure how to describe it, but I suppose the nearest thing I can think of was some alligator I had in South Africa, which again I can't describe. And I'm not going to say chicken, as most people would.

One of the nicest evening surprises was our adventure on the outskirts of town to a tofu restaurant. It was a wooden building with a classy air. Once you've taken your shoes off at the front door, you enter a simple room that reflects the building's exterior. Each table has a hole in the middle with a burner for the tofu. As we sat, my good friend Mark Edwards joined us. He runs all the Nobu kitchens globally, and what a great surprise it was – he hadn't mentioned he would be in Tokyo.

This dinner certainly changed my perception of tofu and what it should be like, in terms of both texture and taste. Once everyone is seated, the waiter pours bean curd into the well in the centre of the table and then closes the lid. When each course is served, he gives the bean curd a stir and it thickens. Then when it's almost there, he adds green pea purée to some and serves it simply scooped out into a bowl. This was rather like the time I went to Pantelleria, an Italian island, and tasted freshly made steaming ricotta. There was no looking back on pre-packed tofu after this, rather like the ricotta. The natural white tofu was served again later with a spoonful of braised Japanese mushrooms.

Tsukiji Market was quite something. If you haven't been and are planning a trip to Tokyo, then you must go. Whatever people tell you, then just multiply that by 10 as it's like no other market. There's a lot of live fish and shellfish, and some species I'd never seen before in my life – and I thought I was quite well informed about fish and seafood. It is fairly normal, it seems, to trade live fish and shellfish, as opposed to fish that may have been on a boat for a couple of days and then kept in a cold store – so you never really know quite how fresh the fish is.

You really need a couple of days to get around the market because, apart from the fish market itself, there's also the tuna auction market, which is the size of a football ground. Back then the endangered bluefin tuna story hadn't come out, so I innocently looked around in amazement at huge tuna weighing hundreds of kilos that had been carefully selected by the fishermen to fetch the best price at auction. Then, once the tuna are laid out in the huge auction room, the potential wholesalers or restaurants use an instrument that looks like an apple corer. They stick this into the tuna to get a sample of the flesh, which they taste for its sashimi-eating and textural qualities. If I had known then what I know now regarding depleting tuna stocks and overfishing by Japanese factory shops, I wouldn't have set foot in the tuna auction area. Yet I did, and I'm glad I did. However, I'm certainly pleased that I'm now better informed, although lots of restaurants still turn a blind eye and don't have a guilty conscience.

Eating and shopping on the edge of the market is also a must. There are some amazing small cafés there that serve all sorts of authentic Japanese dishes, including lots of fish and seafood, of course. Now, there's nothing I don't eat or dislike and, believe me, I've eaten every internal organ and animal and fish going. I don't know if you've ever eaten *nattō*, which is fermented soya bean? Well, I have. It was like chewing a piece of Munster cheese that had matured for a year too long. The Japanese eat this soya bean and *Bacillus subtilis* concoction for breakfast. The Latin element probably describes the taste a bit better. So Tokyo was where something passed my lips that I found totally disgusting and the flavour has stayed with me 20-plus years later.

There are shops selling different grades of bonito flakes and dried loins of bonito that you can shave yourself on these special little bonito-shaving boxes with ultra-sharp blades to get your desired thickness of flakes. Of course, I had to buy one with a loin of bonito and some lovely handmade ramen noodle bowls from the shop next door, which I still have and use a lot today. And I also had to buy an extra suitcase for all this stuff. I kept being left gifts in my hotel room, which was very generous but there was literally no room in my luggage for them.

While I was wandering the city, I stumbled across a fishing tackle shop and back then my fly-fishing addiction was relatively new. Now this tackle shop was something else. It was pretty small, but the walls had intersliding hidden sections, so behind each wall of tackle were two more walls full of stuff – very clever and something I'd never seen before. Why don't more tackle shops do that? You'd get more 'sweeties' for your money and there would be more choice for customers.

My friend Steve Edge had been banging on about this particular weight sage fly rod that he'd bought, which in fly rod terms is the lightest rod you can buy. It really ups the sport and excitement when you're fishing for small trout. I asked in the shop, as back then the exchange rate was pretty good, and was pointed in the direction of a rod rack that had all the latest sage rods and at two-thirds of the price back home. Of course, I had to buy the reel to match, a new line, some flies and a few sea bass lures I'd clocked on the sliding wall display. I didn't go to Tokyo planning to fish or even visit a tackle shop, but the fishing addiction travels around the world with you and you'll always find something of interest that you think you might need.

The chefs in the kitchen got wind of the fact that I was a fishing nut. They said that they had a little surprise for me and to meet them in the hotel lobby at 6.00am. I was intrigued, but guessed the surprise was connected with fishing after a little tip-off. They drove me for what felt like hours on end to Ashinoko Lake, near Mount Fuji, which was in fact an hour and a half's drive out of Tokyo. We left early in the morning, and they handed me a beautiful gift of a British-made fishing flat cap and a box of trout flies. We arrived at the lake where you couldn't see more than 10m (33ft) in front of you. By the time we'd tackled up and had a Japanese breakfast at the hotel there, the mist had lifted and Mount Fuji was crystal clear.

I couldn't wait to put my new purchases to use, although the little feather-light rod isn't designed for casting in big old lakes. But I thought I should at least try and christen her in the country of purchase. Well, my Japanese kitchen companions nailed a couple of trout and laughed at me trying to cast my new little wand. Just as I was about to give up and switch rods to something a bit heavier and fit for purpose, I hooked into a little trout, which made them crack up even more. The little trout came aboard the boat and was quickly returned. We'd had fun at least and a fair day's unexpected fishing on an amazing lake with a few decent-sized trout in the bag, but the highlight for me was the location in crystal-clear water below the mountain and, of course, playing with my newly acquired toys from the tackle shop.

Dancing prawns

Serves 4–6

The small native prawns you get in the UK are ideal for this dish, and if you spend time on the seashore you can catch them yourself in drop nets, as I used to do as a kid growing up on the Dorset coast. You may also be able to buy very fresh prawns from a fishmonger, but as you are eating them raw they need to be ultra-fresh, not frozen and defrosted. Alternatively, you could serve the prawns boiled. Let your guests eat the cooked flesh with some homemade mayonnaise, then, after they have finished peeling and eating the prawns, deep-fry the shells, scatter them with flaky sea salt and serve them, too. Either way, it's a fantastic, waste-free way to eat prawns.

200–250g (7–9oz) small, raw (preferably live) or cooked prawns (in the shell)

Vegetable or corn oil, for deep-frying

Cornish flaky sea salt

Yuzu, ponzu or good-quality soy sauce, to serve

OK, so if you are brave enough and want to have a go at proper dancing prawns, peel them alive, place the flesh on a small serving plate and serve to your guests, letting them pour over the yuzu, ponzu or soy sauce themselves. Heat about 8cm (3¼ inches) of oil in a deep-fat fryer or other suitable heavy-based saucepan to 160–180°C (325–350°F). Deep-fry the shells for 2–3 minutes until crisp, stirring with a slotted spoon occasionally, then transfer to a plate with kitchen paper and scatter with sea salt.

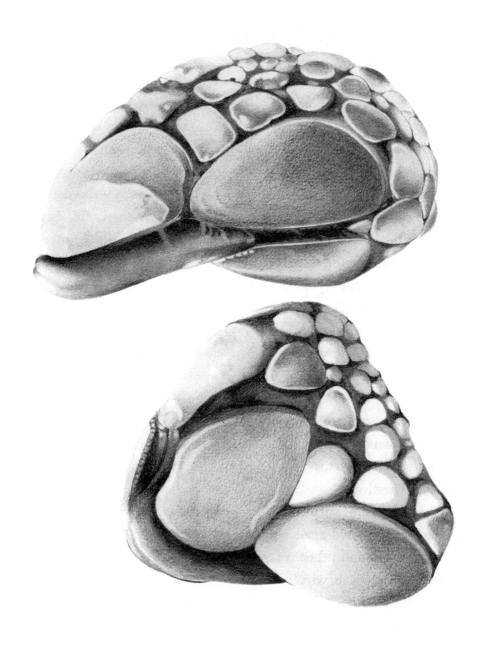

Losing my virginity in Ireland

So, the week after I handed my manuscript to my publisher, I visited Peter Hannan in Ireland. We have fished on the River Moy several times in different spots, even the famous Ridge Pool in Ballina, County Mayo, which has a great reputation for consistent salmon, but we've never caught a damned thing except for trout.

I flew from Exeter to Belfast, where Peter met me, and we drove down to the west where we would be fishing for the day on the private Mount Falcon stretch on the River Moy. We brainstormed new meat cuts and various other fishing chit-chat on the way, and obviously the subject came up once again of me never ever catching a salmon in Ireland.

We stopped by Tiernan Bros tackle shop in Foxford, which we had visited before to pick up our fishing licences and tags, so we didn't have to mess around in the morning and could get straight on to the river. We settled into a few pints of Guinness before dinner in the Mount Falcon hotel bar where we were staying, just across the road from their stretch of the Moy. After a full Irish breakfast next morning, we headed over the road to meet Mike, who would be our gillie for the day. Sadly, the water was too high to fly-fish and still a bit brown from the storms in the last week.

I was pleasantly surprised at what a gloriously sunny day it was, as I had half expected a call from Peter saying that the fishing was off. Mike took us on the boat with our kit to a stretch a mile down the river. There was no wind, the sun was shining and, apart from the high brown water, we felt we stood a chance of breaking the long Irish salmon silence.

We were using fairly heavy Flying C lures (abbreviated from flying condom, as they are a pretty crude, rubber-bodied spinner with a spinning blade), which have successfully out-fished other classic spinners and lures for decades. Mike had brought along a couple of rods set up with floats and worms, which neither Peter nor I are keen on, but it's a pretty traditional method on Irish rivers. Twenty or so garden worms are secured to a bunch of hooks below a float, which is then drifted down the river on the current. Coloured prawns are also commonly used. We prefer the fly and spinning method – but, when your gillie says put the fly rod back in the boot of the car, you have to listen, as he is as keen as you are for you to catch fish by whatever method necessary.

Within the first 45 minutes I had hooked two salmon and lost them both, just as Mike was about to lift the landing net under them. Well, that was slightly disappointing – but equally encouraging, as we knew there were fish in the river and the adrenaline was going. I suggested to Mike that it was time to change colours, as Peter had just landed a fish on a red Flying C.

Mike went off to lunch and left us to it, just after Peter had landed yet another fish, and within 15 minutes I had another one, which Peter successfully got the net under. That put a smile on our faces: it was the long-awaited moment when I lost my virginity in Irish waters – even if it was on a flying condom.

Two of Peter's fish had swallowed the hooks down, so weren't really returnable (as we did with the other fish). So, as we were staying in a hotel and hadn't brought a barbecue, their destiny was the local smokery near where Peter lives in the north.

After fishing, we had a quick shower and a couple pints of Guinness, then headed into Ballina to try out a new Asian restaurant (which wasn't half bad). Then we strolled down the main high street to our favourite watering hole, Doherty's, which is right next to the Ridge Pool. On our ten-minute walk we walked past 20 bars. I said to Peter, 'How do these places survive, as they are all empty?' He said that there are 52 bars in Ballina and, yes, 'God knows how.'

We were greeted at Doherty's by Ed Doherty – who Peter knew well from many fishing trips over the years. Like a lot of bars in Irish fishing towns, there is a tackle counter in the actual bar. I loved this idea, even if Ed's bar did have tackle and lures that looked like they'd been there for decades. When we mentioned the number of bars in town, Ed said, 'There used to be 92, you know, and they would have been a part of people's houses: live upstairs and operate a bar to live on in the living-room space.' Well, Ed doesn't live upstairs, but always seems to be serving in his bar (when he's not fishing or shooting), which is clearly his passion. So we ended the night toasting my lost virginity with Ed and a bottle of Paddy whiskey.

Index

〜〜〜〜〜〜

About the illustrations

I started chatting to the illustrator Nettie Wakefield at the bar in the Groucho Club one night after a few negronis. She asked me if I'd liked her piece for the show. Well, negronis can get the better of you and suddenly creep up, and it was then that I twigged it was Nettie and that she had a drawing in our Art Wars show at my gallery at the Tramshed. When my head was clearer a few days later, I asked Nettie if she would be up for drawing some fish for a book I was writing. She agreed, and so since then I've been sending fishing photos to Nettie and she gets back to me extremely pronto with fantastic drawings.

About the illustrator

Nettie Wakefield (b.1987) is a British artist based in London. She gained a Masters degree in Drawing at Wimbledon College of Arts and was shortlisted for the Jerwood Drawing Prize in 2013. In 2015, her work was showcased at Banksy's 'bemusement park' project, Dismaland, in Weston-super-Mare, Somerset. She has had solo exhibitions in London and Los Angeles.

List of illustrations

Author's acknowledgements

Thanks to all my fishing buddies for teaching me a thing or two, contributing to having the more than occasional blank, adding to the lunch-time and post-fishing fun, encouraging me to buy kit I don't really need and of course for guiding the fish into the landing net on occasion.

To learn more about conservation in fishing, please watch the documentary *The End Of The Line* (2009) and go to bluemarinefoundation.com

Illustrations opposite, clockwise from top left: Nigel Hill, Robin Hutson, Oliver Rampley and Stephen Webster.

About the author

Celebrated chef, restaurateur and food writer Mark Hix is known for his original take on British gastronomy. After 17 years as Chef Director at Caprice Holdings, he opened his first restaurant in 2008 – the distinguished HIX Oyster & Chop House in Smithfield. It was followed by HIX Mayfair at Brown's Hotel, HIX Selfridges, Hixter City, HIX Soho and two chicken and steak concept restaurants, Tramshed in Shoreditch and Hixter Bankside. Located below Tramshed is the HIX ART gallery, while Mark's Bar, with a cocktail list full of historical curiosities, can be found below HIX Soho and Hixter Bankside. In 2015, Mark opened his first stand-alone Mark's Bar at The Old Vic, and in 2016 he partnered with Damien Hirst to open Pharmacy 2 at Newport Street Gallery in Vauxhall.

Outside London, in Mark's native Dorset, are HIX Oyster & Fish House and HIX Townhouse, a boutique guest house, both in Lyme Regis.

Mark's cookbooks include *Mark Hix on Baking, Hix Oyster & Chop House* and *British Regional Food*, which received a Guild of Food Writers' Award and the André Simon Book Award – Special Commendation, *British Seasonal Food*, which was named The Guild of Food Writers' Cookery Book of the Year in 2009, and *Mark Hix The Collection*.

In 2017, Mark was appointed MBE for services to hospitality.

Find out more about Mark at www.hixrestaurants.co.uk

@MarkEHix